A book about personal finances, decisions, a~~~~ ~~~~~~~
It is about *having your cake and eating it too*.

Every decision either *costs* us or pays us.

DOLLAR DECISION$

ANDRE BOYD

HAP & HARPER
PRESS

Printed in the United States of America

First Printing, 2018

Hap & Harper Press

Florence, South Carolina

_____

This book is dedicated to you and your quest for good health, happiness, and riches. May this book be the seed that grows your *Wealth and Plenty*.

To my parents, who saw me as a worthy investment.

TABLE OF CONTENTS

If you don't read anything else in this book, *please* read this.

This book was written because I needed it. I remember the Tuesday that I made the decision to change. Not only for the better, but for the best. And for me, the reason wanting a change wasn't all about the bill collectors waking me. It wasn't even about the "repo man" driving his wrecker up during a cookout one afternoon to repossess my Honda Accord. Strangely, it wasn't even at the point of coming home after a long day at the job only to wonder why *none* of the light switches would work. There's no other feeling than stepping into that quiet darkness and knowing that you are a day late and more than a few dollars short. Bank account on empty. No options.

I was financially and emotionally exhausted, disgusted with my lifestyle and disappointed with my own decisions. Telling myself I deserved more than I had; when I had exactly what I deserved: a little less than nothing.

At that point, I realized that I'd been through too much to finish both broke and broken. That was the day I vowed to myself that I would never be broke again.

Later I learned I was not the first. Plenty of people have allowed poor decisions to wreck their finances. And even while working two and three jobs, we place ourselves back into this paycheck-to-paycheck lifestyle.

Anyway, that *Tuesday*, I made the decision to change my life. To organize it beginning with my financial situation. As I became more focused, I began to understand that I didn't need magic or a miracle. I needed discipline. Soon I learned that my poor money management was a direct result of my poor decisions, bad habits and daily routines. It wasn't a money problem at all. I allowed my decisions to mismanage my entire life.

Well, enough about my mess-ups.

How much are your dreams worth?

No, I don't mean *how many dollars*. I am asking how much are your dreams worth? Are they worth getting up at 5 a.m. every morning? Are they worth wearing the same two pairs of shoes rather than buying new ones? Are they worth limiting the time you spend with your so-called best friend?

How much are you worth?

How much are your children worth?

Your grandchildren?

Your spouse or significant other?

Financing the lives we want comes with a price, but it is more than worth it. Until we commit to making necessary changes, we will continue living lives we don't want.

    This book wasn't written by a certified public accountant or professional financial advisor. I, possibly like many of you, have made millions and lost it. Little to show for it. I don't know if it was serendipity or purpose, but this beautiful mess I found myself in was one of the best and worse things that could have happened to me. And what I learned from that experience could help me get out of any financial disaster.

I am glad to share a few thoughts to help you to take a closer look at your decisions and at every dollar they are connected to.

The Wealth and Plenty Prescription

There is a good life waiting for you. When you believe this with every bone in your body, you will either find this life or build it for yourself. Before you begin your journey, the following strategies will make the challenge more than manageable.

Write a list of your current monthly expenses. Then, write down your expenses for the last twelve months. This shouldn't be difficult if you usually use your debit card. Look at your statement online or find a paper copy.

Calculate your net worth. Your net worth is simply your assets minus your liabilities. Make a list of everything you actually own, that's paid in full. Not Rent-A-Center couches and the ancient iPhone 3GS you are still making payments on.

Take all of your credit cards and burn them. Do not cut them up or throw them away. Burn them. This will help you internalize the deadening power of debt.

Inventory everything you belong. Sell the items you do not need or want. Social media sites can help make this a simple and painless task.

Eliminate everyone in your circle that has a lower financial or emotional net worth than you desire. Every relationship either inspires you or tires you. All in the same, every relationship is either an asset or a liability. Everyone either deposits or withdraws. Write a list of the five individuals you choose to encompass your circle for the next year.

Spend time with wealthy, emotionally healthy people. Broke people breed broke and brokenness only. Remove clubs, bars, and blocks from your pastime's routine. Few million-dollar contracts are found in these places.

Give up gossip and negativity cold turkey. Don't speak it. Don't listen to it.

Do not use profanity. Don't tolerate it in your company. Profanity is called "cursing" for a reason. It is the opposite of "blessing." Our words carry so much power.

A five-dollar mentality never buys a one-million-dollar lifestyle.

Understand that wanting a better life and wanting an easier life isn't always the same desire.

It doesn't matter whether or not people had the right to give up on us. This is not a good reason to give up on our dreams.

Get three jars or containers. Put a dollar in one. Pennies in another. Silver in the last. Spend no less than 30 minutes finding all change in your pockets, drawers, couch, car, etc. Begin collecting. Pay attention to the value of each coin.

Drink at least two glasses of water daily.

Make yourself move bowels every morning, no matter what. Drink a warm beverage if you can't.

Break your bad habits, whatever they are. They will rob you. If liquor owns you, quit. If reality shows dictate your behavior and schedule, quit watching.

Limit phone calls. Take only emergency calls before work or school. Do not take phone calls after 8 pm. Period.

Limit TV to 5 hours per week, preferably on weekends only. When you are serious about changing your life tremendously, stop watching TV.

Get up out of bed two hours before you report to school or work. Don't be dollar *and* time poor. Use your abundance of time as leverage for money and performance.

Do something fun daily, if even playing a game on your mobile device. When you become more disciplined, walk in and out of a store without a purchase. Shoot at the gun range. Fly a kite or drone. Throw yourself deep into a hobby or creative project.

Keep options. Don't make a habit of stressing over one person, place, or thing.

Never compare your life to someone else's particularly if they aren't going where you intend to go.

Write a life plan including:

A.   Financial Goals

B.   Career Goals/Education and Training

C.   Health and Wellness

D.   Leisure and Happiness

E.   Hobbies and Creative Projects

F.   Life Purpose- contributions to society

Or Complete the "*Wealth and Plenty* Plan Worksheet"

Always take a lunch break. Always. Never sit in the office or on the line. Take a walk. Get out. Your body functions in quarters. Your body needs to reset at lunch. This will increase your productivity and prepare you for the evening's rest.

Don't order out every day for lunch. Bring your lunch from home as often as you can. This will more than likely increase your savings by 175%+. These sacrifices will matter when you can afford to eat several meals in Paris and fly back to a home that is 100% paid for.

Dream big, but think small. Decide what you are willing to do without to ultimately get what you want from life.

Remind yourself often that no decision is reversible.

Life is a business. Don't just handle it. Manage it.

The Dollar Decision Philosophy

Choices flood our days forcing us to make decisions. And lots of them. Most of us make hundreds of decisions before we even hear our first "good morning." Research suggests that the average adult makes 35,000 conscious decisions per day. Take Sarah for instance.

Sarah awakes to the sound of her alarm. Then, she decides to go back to sleep. After pressing "snooze" five or six times, she finally decides to get out of bed.

The flats or the heels? She goes with the heels. They go better with the pencil skirt.

She's running late but needs coffee. She decides to speed through the yellow traffic light while listening to the Breakfast Club on 105.1 Radio.

The *Dollar Decision Philosophy* suggests that while all of our decisions affect our lives, our decisions directly impact our finances. Every decision we make will either cost us or pay us. Every choice has a value, a dollar amount assigned to it.

Suppose we *do* make 35,000 decisions a day. At $100 per decision, theoretically, we either earn or lose 3 and ½ million dollars a day.

Surely, all decisions are not created equal. Choosing between eating pancakes or grits would not be a costly decision for most. But for those with allergies and threatening health issues, it could.

Deciding to use separate banking accounts as newlyweds could breed distrust and later cause marital problems.

Making the decision to finance a $25k wedding only to finish paying it off five years after your divorce.

Deciding to waste tens of thousands of dollars to prove you are not the same underachiever you were in high school.

What about the guy who learns on his lunch break that his girlfriend is pregnant? Not only has he spent lots of money on his girlfriend, but he doesn't know how to tell his *wife* he has to spend even more. *Dollar Decisions*.

Deciding to spend $12,000 to learn a new skill that increases your income by $1000 a month.

Suppose you've always wanted to visit California. You could spend your hard-earned $1500 *now* or you could wait 14 months until your job flies you there for training. All expenses covered.

The wannabe-miser who wants to save money by building his own garage. Being that he is inexperienced, he makes a costly mistake that results in a severe leg injury. Long story short, on top of the house damages, he had no health insurance. Medical bills are sky-high and the poor guy was fired for missing too many days from work. *Dollar Decisions*.

Principle #1: Every decision is a *Dollar Decision*. Every decision will either cost us or pay us.

Our thinking controls our spending. If this is true, we must make every great or small decision with our finances and desired lifestyle in mind.

Principle #2: A dollar's only purpose is to multiply our options, by increasing our *Wealth and Plenty* which ultimately improves every dimension of our lives.

Money is meant to be invested, not wasted.

Principle #3: *Wealth and Plenty* are not obtained by everyone; they can be obtained by anyone disciplined and determined.

Along with our mindset and thinking, we must develop strong positive habits and routines that not only generate wealth by attracting dollars but lifestyles that help maintain what we acquire (or earn).

Don't make excuses. Make the best use of your resources.

Maybe it is inexplicable, but I still ask myself.

How can a trumpet have but three keys, yet Miles Davis played everything differently than anyone has, ever? How could Grandmother take two lemons, table sugar, and tap water and make the best lemonade to come out of anyone's kitchen?

How does one become, as we say, filthy rich? When every person ever born or died came and left the same way. Broke and empty-handed.

How does one married, well-to-do, stay-at-home mother complain about not having enough time? Yet, there is another single-mother of five who still finds time to attend her son's football games between her two jobs. Time gives us one day to use as we will every 24 hours.

Principle #4: Wealth is a house. It must be built, secured, and maintained.

One the biggest lies that we tell is that wealth will care for itself. Wealth is no different from a vehicle, needing gasoline and upkeep; it is not much different from an infant or a beloved pet. Wealth must be attended to thoughtfully and regularly. It is documented that 70% of wealth is lost by the second generation. And look at this:

Ninety percent (90%) of wealth, just 10% away from all, is lost by a family's third generation.

This means I could leave millions to my children and it is a strong possibility that they will lose the wealth and return to poverty if it isn't properly managed.

Principle #5: Never make "poor" decisions.

We may not always make the best decisions but we must always make good ones. Every decision maximizes or minimizes our current and future opportunities.

We are making choices that affect our unborn offspring. You are making decisions today that will affect the spouse you haven't even met yet. We don't need to make bad decisions because we can't afford to.

CHAPTER 1
MORE MONEY,
MORE OPTIONS

DOLLAR DECISION$

CHAPTER 1
MORE MONEY, MORE OPTIONS

Moolah.
Paper.
Dinero.
Bands.
Cash.
Benjamins.
Dead Presidents.
Dough.
Bread.
Coins.
Money.

I can do this all day.

The Bible says, "Money answers all things," but also says "for the love of money is the root of all evil." One songwriter says love can't be bought while another says, "Cash Rules Everything Around Me, CREAM, get the money, dollar, dollar bill Y'all." Regardless of our many differing views on money, the reality is- *it* is necessary.

Money is a tool, nothing more. You increase your money to increase your options. You increase your options by increasing your resources. We shouldn't want *enough* money just for the sake of having dollars. It isn't about simply being able to buy things or having bragging rights. Having money isn't about impressing people. Accumulating and maintaining an abundance of money is all about using our *financial* health to improve our quality of life, happiness, and physical health or what I call *Wealth and Plenty.*

MONEY LETS US CHOOSE "BOTH."
We will cover this theme later in our discussion, but for many of us, (at least for me) we seem to have developed a mindset of "this-or-that." Perhaps our circumstances or upbringing conditions us to *have to choose* between the things we need most. You shouldn't have to choose between working an extra shift to meet your monthly bills and your daughter's PTA meeting. We don't have to choose between paying the light bill and the water bill. I don't have to choose to pay my property taxes rather than paying for my wife's birthday gift or my child's medication. Should I continue to work 20 extra hours a week and miss

out on a life of precious moments that will never come again? Options.

You *can* have your cake and eat it too.

Always have at least two cakes. Have options.

When we adopt a mindset of the dollar-wise person, we build a nice savings account and a strong retirement account. Our money buys all of our needs and most of our wants. Options. When financially fit people have to choose between a nice house and good conditioned vehicle, they choose *both*.

MONEY IMPROVES THE QUALITY OF TIME.

Would you agree that life is short? Would you agree that time is valuable?

Even the wealthiest person in the world is given the same denomination of time daily:

Twenty-four hours.

One thousand, four hundred and forty minutes.

Eighty-six thousand and four hundred seconds.

Money gives us the option of "buying time." Of course, we can't buy or save time, but with the right resources, we are able to have a lifestyle that makes the most of the time we are given. Whether we spend an hour working a minimum wage job or spend that hour playing golf, we have that hour. How we spend our time is usually determined by what our lifestyles afford us. When someone has an abundance of money, work is not the reason they wake up.

To make the *Dollar Decisions* that pay us both money and options, we must develop a wealthy mindset.

CHAPTER 2
CHANGE YOUR MIND

DOLLAR DECISION$

CHAPTER 2
CHANGE YOUR MIND

THINK ABOUT THIS.

Do you have a millionaire mindset or a five-dollar mentality?

If you won 5 million dollars today, how would your life change? Some would spend it as fast as they could on shoes or designer fashions. Others would buy monstrous houses and exotic luxury automobiles. Many would buy a series of vacations and a bucket list or two. And then, few would spend wisely, save money, invest some and give most of it away. Unfortunately, everyone will not be a millionaire. In fact, most will not because their thinking won't allow them. Our thinking controls our spending. The way we see money impacts how we manage it. Our pockets will remain empty if we continue thinking that money's only purpose is to be spent. Whether we accept it or not, it is a universal financial law that wealth attracts wealth. Money attracts yet more money while even the hands of "broke" people repel money. Why is this?

Money isn't evil. It isn't stubborn. Dollars do exactly what they are told. Dollars are like children: They go where they are cared for.

WEALTH AND PLENTY MINDSET	FIVE-DOLLAR MENTALITY The "Broke" Mentality
WILL DO WHAT NO ON ELSE DOES TO GET WHAT NO ONE ELSE HAS	WILL GIVE ANYTHING TO GET WHAT EVERYONE ELSE HAS
GET PAID FOR AND BY THEIR HABITS	THEIR BEHAVIOR COSTS THEM; PAY TO SUPPORT THEIR HABITS
FIND SOLUTIONS	FIND FAULT; MAKE EXCUSES
ARE MOSTLY CONCERNED WITH VALUE	ARE ONLY CONCERNED WITH COST
WANT TO BE INFLUENTIAL	WANT TO LOOK IMPORTANT
INVEST IN ASSETS THAT CREATE MORE MONEY	GO BROKE BUYING MORE AND MORE LIABILITIES

The five-dollar mentality thinks: The more money I make, the more money I spend.

This type of thinking focuses on buying liabilities on credit rather than cash cows and assets that generate more dollars.

Impulsive buying.

Self-gratifying.

Non-goal setting.

Irrational thinking.

Materialistic.

The five-dollar mentality.

Changing from this way of thinking is mandatory to be capable of making true *Dollar Decisions*.

Fight the Feeling: *Think carefully, not emotionally.*

The Cost of Emotions
Human emotion is a complicated world all by itself. Our emotions can cost us. To properly manage money, one must first master the emotions. I will be the first to admit, it is often so challenging that it can be exhausting.

We find ourselves working overtime in overdrawn relationships only to be paid no attention. We risk our feelings and our hearts take the losses. Most of our friendships and acquaintances are liabilities; yet they are worth more than we are willing to pay. Our emotional equity is seldom reciprocated. We have loved so badly that we have sacrificed all we've earned to please someone who could not care any less about us. We file emotional bankruptcy only to be left empty. But debts must be paid and all things come with a cost. Love, Happiness, Emptiness, Success, Good Health, Bad Health and even Heartbreak. Everything.

The Psychology of Happy

Our bodies were designed to deal with stress naturally. Endogenous drugs are drugs your body makes naturally in small quantities for its non-biochemical use. Like Oxytocin, it is the love hormone. That good feeling you get when sharing affection. When you hug someone or when someone kisses you. It is produced when you pamper your German Shepherd or British Shorthair kitten. Serotonin is the "happy hormone." It's the hormone that your body produces that makes us feel happy. Spending money gives us these same feelings!

No, that's *not* good.

Never rely on your emotions to make your decisions. Emotions are mostly meant to signal danger. The problem comes is when they misguide you. Misguided emotions make you walk away from the job that you were born for. Emotions can make you walk away from the one that was born for you. Emotions can tell you 'it's over' when the best is yet to come. Emotions will tell you it is time to quit, because you don't "feel" ready. Emotions can make us feel right in the wrong person's arms. Feelings can fool us into making comfortable, safe decisions keeping us imprisoned in mediocrity. Being okay with just being average. You are not average. You're better than that. Again, don't let your emotions make decisions for you.

WE ARE GIVEN LIFE.

Our lives were brought forth without our consent.

WE CREATE A LIFESTYLE FOR OURSELVES.

A lifestyle is built.

BUILD YOUR OWN LIFESTYLE.

A lifestyle is built with three things:

1 Your choosing.

2 Your thinking.

3 Your earning.

With our health, we are what we eat. The same applies to our finances. We are what we buy. Our spending habits are not a result of our circumstances. Our finances are results of our behavior.

You only live once, so *act* like it. Will your current behavior get you to the future that you desire? What has your current thinking made you besides "broke?"

The You Only Live Once (YOLO) way of thinking. The five-dollar mentality wants it all now. People with this way of thinking have behavior that robs them all day, every day. They say, "I can't take it all with me." Then, they go and spend what they don't have as if they will miss out on life. In reality, they are missing out on the prosperous life they could have, if they only understood sacrifice.

YOLO has its own set of principles which often leads to misfortune and poverty.

Forget the YOLO lifestyle. You will have another chance for most things. Aside from your birth, your death, and first impressions, many opportunities will resurface.

This applies to all areas of life. Why go further into debt for a $3500 vacation? Spain has been there for 505 years and I suppose will be there when you save up $3500. YOLO is a coping mechanism. It justifies foolish, irrational behavior.

I have a personal rule for YOLO. Eighty percent of my deliberate spending must be on assets, not experiences that make me feel good. Aside from debt, bills and the like, most of the things I purchase must be able to either generate cash itself or to be repackaged and resold. I can't repackage and resell a trip to the Bahamas or six cruises a year.

Change your mind! Think differently.

Form good habits and routines.

Nothing just happens. Not even *Poverty*. And certainly not *Wealth*.

While we tend to be products of our environment, success and wealth is almost always a direct connection with discipline. The Wealthy understand it isn't enough to want or dream about things.

They are so disciplined that they build habits and routines into every day of their lives that they have no choice but to yield money, good health, and happiness.

By 5 a.m. I make my bed immediately after waking. Everyday. Period. No exceptions.

I cook breakfast daily. Routinely, I wash, dry, and store dishes and utensils immediately after eating. I never head to work with dishes in the sink. Clean or dirty. This isn't just a matter of cleanliness. It is a matter of discipline. It is a habit that I deliberately developed to help bring order to my life. And as I form one good habit, I begin developing another. I continue until working becomes effortless and productivity and creativity become instinct.

Let's skip the science behind habits. Why not keep it simple? There's this neurological loop that builds and controls a habit. In our minds, there is a cue, a routine, and a reward. This is all it takes to create a new habit. As we continue a routine behavior, it becomes easier to do. If you repeat an action or behavior 21 to 60 days, it is more likely to form a habit. This works for good habits as well, except the reward is not always as tangible.

Consider this question before making every decision: *Where do I want to go in life?* Every action must intentionally get you closer to your destination. Your values will give your dollars direction, but your behavior is what moves them.

What bad habits are standing in the way of your escape from debt?

What habits are you willing to develop to bring you closer to the lifestyle you desire most?

I challenge you to write down one behavior that you would like to eliminate from your life and one good habit you would like to form. I dare you to do it today.

How Broke Are You?

How bad is your financial condition? Ballpark figures and guesses don't help much in a critical financial situation. You need to know exactly where you stand financial so you can know exactly what to do to get out of this mess. Don't you ever feel that you are unworthy or any less of a person because of your current financial condition. Many have had life-threatening challenges that shook their faith and their finances. Whether you experienced job loss or the loss of a child, you can recover from these circumstances. Our decisions could have placed us here or not, but our *Dollar Decisions* will get us out. Through this all, remember that you too deserve better.

Earning

Go and find your paystubs. Go online to print out the direct deposit credit amounts. Get your exact income amounts from somewhere. Have your human resources person help you if necessary. If you have a spouse or significant other who contributes to the household, get their pay information as well. Go back 12 months or as far as you can, but no less than 6 months.

Track your spending.

Go through your house or through your car. Find out where you placed all of the bills you got in the mailbox. If you receive bills electronically through email, print them and place them on your table. If you have student loans, rent, mortgage, car payments, credit card bills or light bills, everything you owe. Bring it all out. If there are outstanding debts that you owe and you think the creditor has forgotten about it, pull it out. Everything. Even late alimony and child support payments.

Write a list of every debt you owe with the dollar amount next to it. Make a note next to the ones you are currently on and note the ones that you are a little behind on and how much. If you have credit accounts, call the creditor or collections agency and find out what the "payoff amount" is.

Write it down.

For next 30 days, write down your expenses on paper. Do not begin using an app, just you. You need to internalize your current condition. Include every single purchase with cash, debit, or credit.

Add the totals by day, week, and month. Carefully review your spending.

The Freedom Formula= PESSI+G

(Planning, Earning, Saving, Spending, Investing + Giving)

Planning

Your financial life has never been as important as it is today. What do you want out of life? What type of lifestyle is worth waking up and working hard for? Life is not about just paying bills.

You need more than just a "roof over your head."

You want more than just a car that can "get you from Point A to Point B."

Surely, you want to do more than just "live comfortably."

Do this one thing for me. Take a moment and really think about what your idea of a perfect day would be and literally write it down. Now, imagine what your *dream week* would look and feel like and then your *dream month*. Write it down.

You should now know what type of lifestyle you need to build a financial blueprint for.

When making a financial plan, it doesn't have to be several hundred pages long. You could just as easily and effectively write down your plan on a sheet of notebook paper.

The purpose of a financial plan is to keep us focused on our dreams *and* our money goals at the same time. If we modestly want to be somewhat debt-free or if we want to purchase a vacation home on Daniel Island in Charleston, making and spending money with a purpose is likely to get us there.

No two financial plans are alike. We are not all exactly the same. Our needs and desires are different.

What are your short-term financial goals?

What are your long-term financial goals?

Create your Earning Plan. This is how you will finance your dreams and lifestyle of choice.

What is your immediate plan of for earning income?

Based on my value and experience, what specific minimum wage will I accept? Will it be $20 an hour? Will it be $100 an hour?

Will you pick up a part-time job at your place of employment or work extra hours? How long will you do this before you find additional sources of income?

Saving and Security Plan

You need to begin saving for security and then saving to grow money through interest and investments.

How much do you pay yourself?

How much do you pay your future self?

How much do you think would need to live for a few months if you lost a job?

Is it $1000? $3000?

Begin saving this amount of money and do not even touch it, except for actual emergencies. And being *broke* or unprepared isn't an emergency.

Perhaps you want security and you want to own a home or an inexpensive reliable vehicle.

Make goals. Write them down. Work towards them.

Spending Plan

What are your rules for spending?
For instance, if it isn't a necessity you can only justify a purchase if it will yield a return of its purchased price. So, if you pay $400 for a camera, make sure you take freelance jobs and generate at least $400 of revenue.

If you make $9 an hour and your meal at the local restaurant cost you $15, you need to ask yourself if it was worth it?

Do not stop living your life; just become aware of every purchase. Whether one dollar or one hundred, know where your money is going. Our spending should be strategic and not spontaneous.

Investment Plan

What are your investment needs?
Do you want small quick returns or are you willing to wait decades and hope for a greater return?
Are you willing to take risks with your money?
Do you want to invest your money or do you want to pay someone to invest it for you?

Giving Plan

What are your values, those things you feel so strongly about?

Do you have causes or issues you feel the need to support? Ones that you want to donate money or time to?

What dollar amounts do you plan to give? Which churches, schools or charitable organizations?

A Dollar for Your Time

Pay. Wages. Salary. Earnings. Income is all the money that *comes in.* Income comes in two ways: as active (working) income and passive (creative) income. Active income is money earned by physically working a job. Passive income is money generated without it being necessary to be physically present to perform the job, service, or exchange of goods. Passive income is what makes and keeps us wealthy.

Let's look at active income for a minute. Do you know how much you actually earn? As an employee, you have agreed to exchange your time for money. Whether it is for $15 an hour, more or less, you expect a fair exchange. You have an agreement with your employer that you get paid for the hours you work. Even if you have a salary, you get paid at a daily rate and yearly amount.

When you were hired, you completed a W-4 form. This is an IRS certificate indicating your tax situation. Your marital status and your allowances. The more the allowances, the fewer the dollars are withheld from your paycheck. If you have fewer allowances, more money will be taken from your paycheck and hopefully refunded to you the following year.

So, how much does your job really pay you?

Your gross income is the amount of money you get paid before voluntary and involuntary deductions. *Voluntary deductions* could include supplemental insurance premiums or a 401k plan. *Involuntary deductions* are not optional. You have no choice. Involuntary deductions take money away from you. The state and federal income taxes. The Social Security every worker must pay, by law. Medicare and so and on. Your net income or net pay is your "take-home pay". This is the amount you actually get.

Income is unmistakably the greatest resource you have to begin getting out of debt, but a regular full- or part-time job is not likely to help you get wealthy. Almost no one has ever become wealthy without the use of passive income.
Passive income isn't instant, but it's automatic.
Passive income happens just because it does.
Passive income brings you a cash flow of dollars without a restriction of time or space.

With passive income, you don't even need to be there and you will still get paid. Passive income ventures tend to require less work. Also, less time and taxes. Passive income multiplies your resources while active income exhausts your resources. Let's just say you're commuting 45 miles a day, spending 8 to 10 hours on your feet. You've lost time, gas, vehicle value, energy, and health.

Again, passive income creates money. Money affords more options. We don't have to choose between the pay and the vacation. Passive allows you to be sick or take off and still get paid.

There is no such thing as "free time." There is always an opportunity to be productive and this form of income helps us do just that.

Lastly, active income is necessary. Making an honest living is honorable. It is. But there are only two major reasons for working for someone else: (1) to build money (capital) and (2) to build understanding (knowledge & skills).

CHAPTER 3
BUDGETING
BUILDS WEALTH

DOLLAR DECISION$

CHAPTER 3
BUDGETING BUILDS WEALTH

Janet's birthday.
Dog food.
Property taxes on the primary vehicle.
Dad's retirement gift.
Ryan's college tuition.
Kinsley's braces.

Which is the one most important expense? They are all priorities and are all arguably of equal importance.

Budgeting helps us get our priorities in order without having to guess or stress about things before or after spending. Our focus is budgeting our dollars, but this strategy indirectly affects our time, health, relationships and other resources.

Budgeting is a basic concept. The whole idea is planning your spending before you even spend a dollar. It's about spending less than you have. There are hundreds of useful apps, websites, and worksheets to help you budget, just search the web. Right now, I just want you to understand the big idea of spending each brown penny and knowing where it goes. Become skilled at tracking your expenses. This may sound like extra work you just don't have time for, but I assure you it's not that difficult once you make this a habit.

Write down your net monthly income. If you get paid weekly or twice a month, write down the month's total or your expected monthly pay. Again, this is your net pay, the amount you actually get after taxes, voluntary and involuntary deductions.

List your expenses. It would be wise to go back a few months to get an idea of what your actual recurring monthly/quarterly expenses are. This will be helpful later when you begin cutting back and saving some money.

Create your budget categories. Every expense should fit into one of two categories: fixed or variable. Fixed expenses tend to be the same each month. Rent, a mortgage payment, insurance, car payment. These tend to be the same. On the other hand, variable expenses change. The water bill, lights/electricity, the mobile phone bill, these could be in the low $70 and at other times $100 or better.

Feel free to be creative, but be concise and specific. Here is an example of my budget categories

Fixed
House
Student Loans
Life Insurance
Insurance (Home & Vehicles)

Variable
Utilities
Water
Lights/Power
Gas
Internet
Mobile Phone
Vehicle Gas
Food/Groceries

After taking a serious look at how much you *actually* make minus how much you spend a month, try to see what you can do without. Make adjustments. You don't have to do this all at once, but if you notice unnecessary purchases and patterns, eliminate.

Begin cutting the "extras." Do you need Netflix, Hulu, Amazon, and YouTube Red along with cable? I can answer that for you. There are a number of free/open source streaming resources available to you. Consider keeping your internet services and finding your public library card. Visit your local library and checkout unlimited DVDs, streaming/download subscriptions, all at no cost. **Terminate cable, satellite, and streaming subscriptions today.**

Convenience is robbing you. Stopping by the fancy coffee shop for breakfast. Eating out for lunch and dinner each day. These are things we do for convenience. Even with demanding schedules, if we were to get up early enough to cook breakfast and prepare meals for dinner a few times a week, it could be a huge saving. There are instances that your time and energy is simply more valuable. This is understandable. Consider washing your own vehicles. Cutting your own grass. Cutting or washing your own hair. Save money in these areas, if possible.

Commitment Checklist

1. Cancel cable and/or satellite and streaming subscriptions.

2. Bag lunch daily. If you need motivation, reward yourself by eating out twice a month.

3. Schedule your sleep to get at least 7 hours a night. Get up early enough to prepare breakfast and lunch at home.

4. Do not purchase canned soft drinks at the grocery store or from vending machines. Drink water or make homemade iced tea or lemonade.

5. Eliminate cigarettes, gourmet coffee, and alcohol from your diet and expenditures.

6. If you must meet friends, meet them for breakfast or at home. Do not spend too much money eating out. Besides, you know you'd probably end up paying for their meal too.

CHAPTER 4
BORROW
RESPONSIBLY

DOLLAR DECISION$

CHAPTER 4
BORROW RESPONSIBLY

Debt and Loans

Let me be the first to tell you that debt is necessary. I won't deny it. We all will owe someone *something* at some point in our lives. I understand that debt and credit can be leveraged in business. I am aware that creditors and business-savvy entrepreneurs can somehow get dollars from debt and even write-off debt as business expenses. As attractive as this sounds, debt doesn't have long-term benefits in our personal finances.

Debt will destroy you. Think it won't. Play around with it and watch what happens. You've seen it destroy homes and communities. The stress debt causes has killed one too many.

Bad credit is easy to get. Hard to get rid of. In all our wishing and wanting, debt just doesn't go away.

Assets and Liabilities

Let's keep this simple. Assets are things you own that benefit you. You've paid for these things and now they should be paying you monetarily or emotionally. Liabilities are things we have that cost us. They are usually those things that we are paying to own. Also, some things that we pursued for assets, later turned into liabilities.

In order to live a life of *Wealth and Plenty*, we must strive to accumulate and maintain more assets than liabilities.

Examples of assets include: land, savings accounts, mutual funds, or a house that is in great condition and paid in full.

Property is a good asset because God is not making any more land. Therefore, its value tends to appreciate (or increase in value) rather than decrease (or lose value) over time.

Examples of liabilities include: car payments, outstanding credit card balances, or student loans

Outstanding credit card balances are seen as liabilities, because they cost you. They continue to deteriorate your potential wealth due to the negative interest on unpaid or slowly-paid debts.

Again, we want assets, not liabilities. Assets *pay* us. Liabilities costs us.

Net worth

What makes a millionaire? Is it someone who's made a million dollars? Of course not. If that were the case, a couple with a combined salary of $100,000 would've become millionaires after 10 years of earnings. Many of us have already made and wasted a couple of million with little to show for it.

A millionaire is a person who has a million dollars in combined assets minus liabilities. If a person has $600,000 in cash equivalents and $400,000 in debt and liability, his or her net worth does not equal $1M or greater.

What is your net worth?

Total Net worth= Total Assets – Total Liabilities

Credit 101

What is credit? Credit involves the ability to borrow money and pay off the debt over time. Notice I used the word "borrow". Whatever is "credited" to us (the borrower) must be returned to the lender (the giver). Credit comes in the form of loans for homes or family cars or in the form of perceived cash on credit cards for in-store or online purchases.

Is credit a bad thing? Not necessarily. But of course, when credit isn't managed properly its debt can cause a financial disaster over time. When used responsibly and strategically, credit can be quite necessary and useful.

Credit is not the same as cash, anywhere. If it is not an emergency, don't charge it. Poor planning is not an emergency.

Credit Report

How good is your credit? Don't assume. Take a look at your credit report and see what creditors see. The Fair Credit Reporting Act requires credit reporting agencies to give you a free copy of your credit report each year upon request.

The three (national) credit reporting agencies are Equifax, Experian, and TransUnion.
Go online and visit www.annualcreditreport.com to retrieve your free credit report. Again, this is free. So, if you paid for it, you got hustled.

Your credit report reveals five main categories:

A.   Personal information and data

B.   Monthly reporting

C.   Defaulted and Delinquent account information

D.   Credit Check Inquires

E.   Public Records (bankruptcies, foreclosures, tax liens and such)

Credit reports cannot report sensitive information, such as medical history, race or ethnicity, and religious affiliations.

Credit Scores

Good credit, bad credit. How is a credit score calculated? What does it mean?
There are several factors included in a credit score. How often we pay our bills on time is one. Whether we have accounts in collections is another. Certain profiles generate specific numbers or scores.

Perhaps you've heard of FICO Scores. FICO is an acronym for the Fair Isaac Corporation. This is the company responsible for their widely-used credit scoring services.

<u>FICO generates credit scores based on the following formula:</u>

35% Payment History
30% Amounts owed
15% Credit History
10% New/Recent Credit
10% Types of Credit

FICO Scores range from 300 to 850.

While there is no official FICO chart, there are ranges that creditors tend to favor. Just to give you a better idea of where you stand, 700 or higher is considered "Good" credit.

Buying a Home

When 4 ½ million houses are listed to be sold, the task of pursuing homeownership can seem overwhelming. But I promise you, you've overcome greater challenges. Buying a house is not impossible. Many have and so can you.

When buying a house, remember you are buying a *home*. Think of the value of this investment. For most, buying a home is the largest purchase we will ever make. And although we don't have to pay for the house all at once, we must buy a house we can actually afford.

Do you want to build or buy a house? Do you have the land? Do you have a down payment? How much do you want your monthly payments to be? Do you need a real estate agent? Will they check my credit? If so, is it good enough to get pre-approved?

You can manage the $700 mortgage payment, but have you thought about homeowner's insurance? Homeowner's Association dues? Property taxes? Just some things to think about as you make plans to own your dream house.

If you want the best deal on your mortgage, and I know you do, you more than likely need an excellent credit score. Well, maybe not excellent, but it needs to be good. Lenders will look at your credit history and your FICO score. Whether a mortgage or a car loan, 40 or 50 points can be the difference between hundreds of dollars a month. Thousands and thousands of dollars over the 15 or 30-year mortgage.

Keep in mind, only apply for mortgages when you are ready. It is fine to complete several applications for mortgages to get a pre-approval, but understand this: Every time your credit is checked by an application you completed, it deducts points from your credit score. Unless the regulations have changed, if all inquiries are completed within a 30-day window, all applications will count as one credit check.

So you've decided to buy a house. What is a mortgage anyway? And how do you get one?

A mortgage is a residential loan that a bank or financial institution offers to purchase a house. The lender, or bank, holds claim and ownership of the house. You make payments and upon fulfilling your obligation as a borrower, you get the deed to the house. If you stop making (mortgage) payments, the house tends to go to foreclosure. You are evicted and the bank sells the house.

Mortgages come in two basic types: fixed-rate and adjustable-rate mortgages (ARMs). Fixed-rates allow the borrower to pay the same rate of interest until paying off the loan. ARMs begin with fixed rates, but as the market/economy changes, so does the interest rate.

Pre-approval

I love to see people house hunt. Even when you don't intend on buying a home immediately, it inspires you to work towards dreams, doesn't it? But that time will come. And when it does, you must be ready. It always helps to have your pre-approval letter in hand. It will give you an idea of the maximum amount of money you have to buy the home. This will save time and letdowns.

The Process

Proof of Income

Suppose you are seeking a bank to finance your house. The person assisting you will ask for at least two W-2s and possibly a certain number of pay stubs. If you do not keep a record of these types of things, you should begin. If you haven't, now's the time to pay your human resources department a visit. They should be willing to assist you in printing out statements and W-2s.

Bank Statements

During your pre-approval meeting, you will have to present bank account statements. They need to know that you can not only make mortgage payments upon approval, but you can cover the closing costs and down payment if needed.

Identity Verification

Bring your driver's license or official ID and social security card. They may request other forms of proof, but these are most common. You will also have to provide your signature verifying your identity and granting permission to initiate the credit check.

Credit Check: It's Good

This is where good credit rewards you. If you have excellent credit, your interest rates tend to be lower as well as your down payment. This will help reduce the amount of your monthly payment as well. This is why it is always important to know your credit score ahead of time. There may even be certain programs available for those with less than stellar credit. For example, FHA-insured loans can be secured by individuals with a credit score less than 600. If you served in the military, you could qualify for a VA loan. This could offer long-term savings and a $0 down payment upfront.

Employment Check

The lender *will* call your job. They want to verify that you have a job and you've maintained stable employment.

Almost Home

The Underwriting Process
After being pre-approved, you find the house you would like to buy.

The bank or lender will complete the process by underwriting. In the underwriting process, several steps will be taken to analyze the institution's risks on the loan. This includes determining if you are capable of making payments to whether the property, including the land, is a worthy investment.

The Appraisal

The bank needs to know that the house and property you want is worth the asking price. It will cost $300 or so for an appraiser to visit the property you want to buy. He or she will look at the square footage, materials used to build and current condition, and improvements made since being built. The appraiser will compare the value of that home to others in the neighborhood. This isn't just a part of the process. The lender needs to know that it can resell this property if you decide to stop paying your mortgage. But this won't happen! You are financially responsible and you are well on your way to enjoy a full life of *Wealth and Plenty.*

Search of Title
The lender will then check to see if there are any existing mortgages, liens, or claims on the property. This protects the initial investment of the lender and protects the long-term interest of the borrower. It could be devastating to work 30 long years to pay off a home only to find out that someone else had full or partial ownership.

Survey

A survey is a drawing or map that notes the attributes of the property. It notes the boundaries, where the property begins and ends. It includes dimensions. It lists the street address and other streets relative to the property. Finally, a survey tends to include a detailed, written report with concerns and recommendations.

Closing Costs

Of course, the fees mentioned and other related costs must be covered to complete the transaction of buying a home. These fees are your closing costs.

Don't be scared. Be prepared.
Here's a rough estimate of what to expect:
Application Fee ($0-$350)
Appraisal ($300)
Attorney fees
Closing/Escrow Fee
Down payment
Title Search & Transfer (if applicable) ($300-$1,000)
Tri-merge Credit Report ($30)

FINANCING A VEHICLE

First of all, buying a brand new car is almost always a poor *Dollar Decision*. But quite honestly, I'm guilty of it. Secondly, if you are able to buy a car with cash without financing, this would be the better option. Go to an auction or purchase a vehicle several years old. I would not recommend exhausting your savings to purchase a car with cash. Cars depreciate too quickly.

The Sell

Car dealers must make a living too, but don't go deeper into debt while financing their next Christmas bonus.

 Focus on the car's actual value rather than the invoice price. The Manufacturer's Suggested Retail Price (MSRP) can and will change. Don't do them any favors. Do your research before even stepping on the car lot. You'll be better prepared to make well-informed decisions.

Always borrow from the bank, if you must. Do not even think of allowing the dealership to finance your car. You'll regret it.

Insurance and Extended Warranties

The first time I bought a car, the dealer asked did I want death insurance on my car. He said, if for some reason I lost my life, they'd pay off the vehicle. They'd do this for only a few dollars a month. Needless to say, I declined his offer. I didn't think I would care about a car after death. Also, I had no wife and children at the time.

The Actual Cost of a Vehicle

Consider how much you'll pay for the vehicle. I once got a "deal" on a luxury vehicle. The services, recurring expenses for repairs and premium gasoline was enough to teach me a lesson on living below my means. I got rid of the vehicle as quickly as I could.

Consider your expected monthly payment. Can you manage it right now? Are the property taxes affordable for you? Maintenance? If you commute 55 miles daily, will you pay more this year for gas with your new SUV than you did with your old small eco-friendly car?

Buying Used

Buying a used car has advantages, one: a reduced cost.

Check the vehicles' history by verifying the VIN number. Look up on Kelley Blue Book or CarMax websites to find additional information about the prospective vehicle.

Search for used cars online. You don't have to make the car lot your first stop.

Don't forget to check with rental companies like Enterprise or Hertz. Also, check the state surplus websites. You can purchase well-kept vehicles at a low price.

When you are ready to purchase a used car, after the test drive, have a certified mechanic perform a diagnosis to make you feel comfortable. And just as importantly, when you make the purchase, do not forget the warranty.

Renting, Buying, Financing to Own or Leasing a Vehicle

What should you do?

Know what's best for your budget, lifestyle, and needs. If you only need a mini-van for summer vacations, rent one as needed. If you only need a pickup truck to move from one house to another, rent or borrow one when that time comes.

Leasing Options

Leasing a vehicle can be a risky option, but could be better for you. You pay to lease or use the vehicle with the intention of returning it to the dealership at the end of a set time period. You then are given the option to buy the vehicle or jump into another vehicle for the next lease.

One advantage of leasing a vehicle is: the monthly payments tend to be less expensive than a traditional finance option. If you like the thought of a different vehicle every one to three years, this could be a suitable option for you.

Four things I'd consider when it comes to leasing are:

1. You're paying for value, not ownership.
2. You are responsible for paying for the leased vehicle's depreciation.
3. You must maintain your vehicle well or it will literally cost you.

4. You must drive less than 12,000 miles or so per year or you could be billed for extended mileage and wear and tear at the end of the lease.

Getting Out of Debt

If you are a little behind with paying your bills, debt collectors will eventually make attempts to contact you. They will try all kinds of ways. They will call several times a day. They will call in the morning or late in the evening. They will even try to spoof you and your own number shows up on the caller ID. Even when we are up to our chins in debt, we still have rights.

The Federal Trade Commission (FTC) enforces the Fair Debt Collection Practices Act (FDCPA). This act says that debt collectors cannot harass, oppress, or abuse you. There are also certain things that collectors cannot legally do.

Third-party debt collectors are not supposed to call your job. This could place you in jeopardy of losing your job.

If family members aren't co-signers, debt collectors should not call your aunt or neighbor to discuss your financial matters.

You can possibly make an arrangement to pay less, but they cannot make you pay more than you owe them. Interest is one thing, but robbery is another.

They cannot call you before 8 in the morning or after 9 in the evening.

A debt collector cannot contact you until a written request for the debt is sent.

Pay Down Debt

Write down every debt you owe with the exact dollar amount. Whether you pay down debt from the smallest to largest amount or tackle the largest first, be strategic. Consider the negative interest. Understand your interest rates and how they increase the total amount of your debt. The longer you take to pay off the debt, the more you will have to pay in the end. If you have a line of credit attached to your checking account and use it to eliminate your debt creatively, great. If a huge blessing of money falls upon you, don't spend it. PAY DOWN DEBT!

CHAPTER 5
REMOVE YOUR
EARNING CAP

DOLLAR DECISION$

CHAPTER 5

REMOVE YOUR EARNING CAP

Our reason for investing is to generate more cash flow which will eventually build the lifestyle that we desire and deserve. As we've already discussed, we cannot depend solely on our day jobs. A paycheck cannot be considered cash flow. I wouldn't even consider it an asset because it isn't reliable. It can be converted into cash with limitations and it is taxed. Moreover, if I do not work, I do not get paid.

 Suppose I make $20 an hour. Out of the 24 hours in a day, I sleep at least at least 8 of those. This leaves me the limited potential of making $320 a day. After taxes, retirement, and voluntary deductions, I can only earn about $244. Of course, realistically, I'd only work 8 hours a day totaling to less than $122 of potential earning per day.

Investing is a way to further *remove the cap* from your potential earning. Income is income. Even if it's just a few dollars here and there. Any additional sources of money of any size add to your wealth.

Where do I begin investing?

If you haven't paid off all of your credit cards and debt, I would begin there. Next, I'd advise anyone who is new to investing to consider the following: *Capital, Risks, Timing, and Liquidity*

Capital
To become successful in investing, you must begin thinking like an investor and not a consumer. Investing requires capital. Capital can come in the form of money, assets, or other types of collateral. Investing will cost something and usually, it's dollars.

Risks
Risks are everywhere. We risk our lives to drive to work or to the supermarket.

You risk your safety as often as you find yourself sitting in a public school-building or a place of worship.

We risk our feelings in relationships. We risk our happiness and our health every single day.

Think of how many of your friends would dress up in their church clothes and risk going to a nightclub where drunk and angry club-goers shot the place up for fun. The frat guy at that Five Points bar, that you didn't even know, that costed you five stitches your freshman year.

When it comes to our finances, particularly our investments, we must be bold enough to take risks with our dollars. But take calculated risks. We mustn't gamble with our money.

There are always wins and losses in personal finance. For instance, we take a risk on a $2000 down payment and pray that our bad credit doesn't still penalize us with a $700 car payment.

Always remember that there can be no wins without risks.

Investing requires giving up something with the hopes of getting something back. Usually, capital, or money, is placed in an investment and the profit is the Return on Investment (ROI).

Timing

Just as with most other pursuits, timing really is everything. Time is just as an important of a factor as capital (money) when investing. We must consider long-term or short-term investments. Which tends to be most risky? Which is more likely to generate more dollars in return over time. Making the decision to sell or trade shares of stock could be a huge gain or huge loss. Keeping an eye on compounding interest. Knowing when to launch your business idea or simply when to call it quits and find a new venture: Time matters.

Liquidity

While some investments allow a place to store capital with tax benefits, if you need cash, which investments allow you to convert assets into cash dollars if you needed them. It's all about getting your money from your investments when you need it.

I don't want to bore you anymore than I have, but it would take hundreds of pages to give a good lesson on investments. Let me give you a crash course. If you want to know more, ask your financial advisor.

Investments 101

When we think of investments we tend to think of five asset classes:

1. Stocks and Shares
2. Bonds
3. Property (Real Estate)
4. Commodities
5. Cash

STOCKS AND SHARES

I am sure you have heard of the Stock Market. It is an interesting playground. Playground or battleground, whichever you prefer. Companies raise money by allowing investors to buy and sell shares of stock. With stocks and shares, it's just how it sounds. You can invest in stock which gives you a "share." It's called a share because you *share* a piece of the ownership. You buy stock in the company. As the company's value increases, so does the value of the stock. And of course, when the company loses value, the value of the stock goes down in price. As the price of stock shares increase and decrease in price, you have the option of holding or keeping the shares. Or, you can trade or sell them. Some allow you the option of earning dividends, which generate immediate income either monthly, quarterly, or yearly. When you get into buying shares of stocks, look for the dividend-bearing stocks first. If you find several publicly-traded stocks that give shareholders a dividend, it's almost like getting paid to buy shares. It is another method of passive income. Please, make a mental note of this. You'll thank me later. I promise.

Market Capitalization

Stocks are generally classified by size: large-cap, mid-cap, and small-cap. Of course, the "cap" is short for "capitalization." Market capitalization is determined by multiplying the number of shares a company offers by the share price. Based on this formula, the market capitalization of a large-cap is $10 billion or more. Mid-cap groups companies less than $10 billion, but more than $2 billion. Small-cap classifies companies with a market capitalization of less than $2 million.

BONDS

Now hear me out. A bond is actually debt. Not yours, but a business's. With this type of investment, you loan your money to a company or a government entity and they agree to pay you back with interest. As interest rates fluctuate, it changes the value of bonds. The longer the term of the bond, the higher the risk tends to be.

Mutual Funds

With this investment option, you give money to a firm or institution. They put your money with other people's money and invest this pool of dollars. Since a large volume of securities are purchased, your fees tend to be lower.

Mutual funds allow you to invest in stocks, bonds, commodities, and cash without having extensive knowledge and expertise.

Do you need a broker?

That's a good question. Let me ask you this: Do you need a barber or mechanic? It depends on your experience and your skill set. It also depends on how much money we are talking. If you are new to investing and you have $25k to buy shares of stock, get some help.

With a broker, you will more than likely be charged fees including commission and possibly more for additional services. I have never bought, traded, or sold stock with the help of a broker. I have always purchased and managed my stock portfolio online. I have made a considerable amount of dollars. The only problem I've ever had was the amount of taxes I had to pay when I sold shares of stock. Other than that, I'm self-taught and enjoy the entire process.

Start investing with $50.

There are too many apps and online brokerages that allow you to buy shares of stock and as many or few as you'd like. I recommend starting there. Invest $50. Buy a few shares of a few different stocks. Watch them for a few weeks. Study how they perform. Follow the market. While you can't predict stock market outcomes, you'll develop an investor's instinct. Trust me, if it's in you, it will come out. If not, leave it to your financial advisor to give you some tips.

Money ain't nothing to play with, but try stock and trade simulations. Download an app. Go online. Practice searching for stocks. Purchase them within the simulation with "fake" virtual dollars and see if you can make sense of it all. Practice may not make perfect, but it will certainly make you better at managing risks. Much better.

PROPERTY
Real Estate Investments

A house is real estate. Owning a home gives tax advantages and offers security. The right house in the right location is always a worthy investment. Also, I suggest owning your home before attempting to purchase other properties to sell.
The wonderful thing about real estate investing is it is affordable. In your leisure, search online for houses for sale in your area posted by a real estate broker for profit. You could even find properties through foreclosure arrangements due to inability to pay mortgage or taxes. Finding properties less than $100,000 or even $10,000 in South Carolina should not be difficult.

What if you didn't want to invest directly in real estate by buying and selling property? Real estate stocks and mutual funds could be an option. But, in most cases you'd get a greater return on investment by owning the property yourself. Investing in pools of properties may or may not generate lots of dollars for you. If you purchased a house or two and rented them out, you could generate cash flow, if you did it correctly. And if you are really a business person, you could use a property as a duplex and multiply your rent from one property.

COMMODITIES

Raw materials. What are they? Gold, sugar, livestock, fruits, vegetables, energy, oil, and the list goes on. Consider your favorite chewing gum, candy bar or latte, the company needed the commodity of sugar. Electricity powers our homes. Oil and gasoline warm our homes and keep our vehicles active. Even our food supply is dependent on these materials during the sowing and reaping phases. Whether you choose to invest directly in commodities or through a company that manages these materials, it could be worthwhile if you know what you're doing. An exchange-traded fund (ETF) is another option. This will give the option of investing in a combination of commodities if you aren't confident in a single raw material investment.

CASH

There are at least 15 ways to invest in cash itself. I have included several throughout the book. Right now, please allow me to focus on one: becoming a lender. I know, you are already a lender when the bank borrows your money. This is true, but this is a little different. As the economy changes, even banks must reduce risks. They cannot just give loans to any and everybody like they used to. This has created a market for normal, everyday people to become "banks." You can invest your money in peer-to-peer lending programs. This money is bundled with other investors and loans are issued to borrowers. You can make money off their debt just as any other lending institution attempts to do. Why is peer-to-peer lending a viable option for borrowers? The loans do not have "unnecessary-necessary" costs included. When banks charge a gang of fees for no legitimate reason, they must generate enough money to pay for brick and mortar real estate, for employees, and for who knows what else. With peer-to-peer lending, everything is managed online. There is no reason to *rob* the borrower. The rates are reasonable. There tends to be less red tape and fewer hassles.

Get Money. Grow money.

Nine Ways to Get Extra Dollars

1. Adjust your withholdings.

A tax refund is simply the extra money we've given to the IRS within a tax year. Rather than filing for your return after the tax year has ended, you could complete another W-4 form. Take advantage of the withholding calculator or speak with your employer to find out how to properly complete the form. This will allow you to take home more money on your paycheck and get your "big payback" throughout the year. Keep in mind, it isn't likely that you will get a large refund as usual, but this extra income can help you with your investments or catching up on eliminating debt.

2. Sell your assets.

Another way to get extra cash is to sell what you are not using. Do you have an extra car in the backyard that you haven't cranked in a year? Or a motorcycle? A video game console or wardrobe? How about a designer pocketbook collection?

The very first time I put this strategy to use I made $3,614.15 in a matter of days. *eBay* was widely used at that time and *still* is. Now there are dozens of social media sites that can help you make money from your mobile device in your leisure. Even *Amazon, Craigslist,* or a local consignment store could help put money into your pocket.

3. Sell Your liabilities.

This could help reduce monthly expenses and costs as well as generate money. If you have a primary or recreational vehicle it could be wise to sell it. Save yourself a monthly payment and save the creditors the time of repossessing the liability. Sometimes even breaking even is a sound *Dollar Decision.* Have someone resume the payments and you go find a used vehicle that you can save up and pay for upfront.

4. Withdraw from your tax-deferred account.

There could come a time when you need several thousand dollars and do not want to get further in debt with a loan. Tapping into your retirement account could provide this financial relief. I would only recommend this if you can guarantee a quick or long-term return on the withdrawal. I am guilty of withdrawing money from my 401k account. But, please know that I not only repaid the $5000 to my retirement account; I made over $5,000 profit with my business venture.

Again, before you consider this option, please count the cost. Normally, you will have five years to repay the money and a little longer if you withdrew the money to purchase your primary home. Also, the money that you put into your retirement account is not taxed. So, when you withdraw money from a retirement account, you may have to report it as income. On top of that, you will more than likely pay a penalty for early withdrawal.

5. Borrow against your insurance policy.

A whole life insurance policy has more than one use. Naturally, the death benefit pays out to your family or beneficiaries in the event of your death. The second use is, the cash value. If you have a policy, you pay premiums or payments to keep it. As you make payments, it builds equity in the form of cash allowing you to borrow from the policy as if it were a bank or retirement account.

6. Make money online.

There are tons of ways to make money online. *Google* it. You can generate actual income from completing surveys or even reviewing demos from up and coming recording artists. Take *Amazon Mechanical Turk (MTurk)* for instance. You simply sign up and after your identity is verified you become an independent contractor. You can search for tasks and upon completion you are paid. Mind you, while the pay for each task is usually less than $0.50, this could still add up. Once, I challenged myself to earning $20 per hour on *MTurk*. While I do not watch television, I purposely completed tasks during commercials while watching television. I did not meet my goal of earning $20 within an hour, but I came very close.

This could be a nice little side hustle.

7. Monetize your creative skills and interests.

Do you cook or bake well? Do you have a professional office job, but you really love sewing? Perhaps you work in a correctional facility or a plant, but you have a graduate degree in English. Use the skills you have to make the money you need. Freelance. Subcontract. Opportunities are out there.

8. Get a part-time job.

If your employer won't give you a substantial raise or promotion right now, get a part-time position at your place of employment. You are already familiar with the politics and work environment. Make extra money there. If this isn't possible, secure a part-time position elsewhere. I have worked a full-time job along with two or three part-time jobs. My only advice is to do this as a temporary effort. Working two or more jobs could have long-term adverse effects. Also, your time is more valuable than money. We must not make the mistake of allowing employers or debt collectors to buy all of our time at a low cost. It simply isn't worth it.

9. Reinvest rather than spending your dollars.

Invest a percentage of your "extra money." Find a way to creatively and strategically grow your dollars. Make them multiply. Create a new income or revenue stream. Start a side or seasonal business. Perhaps you could take a portion of your additional earnings and invest in your financial education. Rather than spending the earned dollars on entertainment, put it towards a subscription or service that helps you become more productive. More prosperous.

CHAPTER 6
SAVING MONEY
TO MAKE MONEY

DOLLAR DECISION$

Chapter 6
SAVING MONEY TO MAKE MONEY

Saving accounts provide security for your dollars. Those dollars provide financial security for your lifestyle. And maybe money won't make you happy, but what you can do with it certainly will.

Perhaps there are few tax advantages for saving money, but there are reasons to store your dollars where they can grow.

Why do I need a bank?

There are dozens of reasons why anyone on a quest for wealth would need a bank. I could take the easy way out and tell you it is simply a *Dollar Decision*. And it is.

As you accumulate wealth, particularly dollars, where would you store it? If you earned $10,000 today, would you keep it in a shoebox under your bed? I hope not.

Those who make sound financial decisions are wise enough to store and insure their money and train those dollars to grow even while not being used.

As we discuss later in the book, banking not only allows better access to your money, but keeps excellent records of your earning and spending should you need to apply for a mortgage. Perhaps you'll need a personal or business loan. For these reasons alone, it makes sense to store your dollars away in a banking institution.

Banks offer convenience. They simplify our lives.

Automatic bill payments and drafting. Direct deposits so you won't have to waste gasoline or time cashing a paper check. Checks at your disposal to write to whosoever you will. Debit cards for swiping or online purchases.

Automate your saving.

The first method of automating your savings may or may not be available by your employer, but I will throw it at you anyway. If you are able, have a portion of each paycheck go directly to your savings account without you even touching it. Preferably, let it be a remote savings account at a bank other than the one you usually visit. Your savings always need to be accessible, but not *easily* accessible.

Banks offer income and increase.

When you deposit your money in a bank, you are paid interest. This interest is paid to you in actual dollars and cents. The banks are not just that nice. They pay you because they use your money to make more money. The bank pulls our dollars to invest in different things from bonds and debt to personal and commercial loans. Don't worry. They will have yours available to you when you are ready to withdraw.

Banks offer security.

The Federal Deposit Insurance Corporation (FDIC) insures us up to $250,000 for depositors. Many home owners' insurance policies only cover about

$200 in the event of theft or destruction of cash stored in a house or vehicle.

Which bank should I choose?

I prefer a local branch. A bank that gives you access to my money whenever I want it, physically or electronically. Also, I made my bank selection based on the availability of ATMs (Automated Teller Machines) in my area. If you choose to open accounts at a bank with few or no ATMs in your area, you may be forced to pay unnecessary charges and fees just to get your own money. Depending on where you live, these fees could be $3.50 or more.

When possible, go with a bank that does not require a minimum balance. Some banks will charge excessive fees for low balances. In these cases, your dollars can disappear monthly if you are not careful.

Stuff the piggy bank.

Collecting coins is a hobby for some and a business for others. Another way to save strategically is to hunt for treasures. I purposely walk the streets and parking lots for coins. Challenge yourself to collect spare change and loose dollars. Check with your local bank or credit union to see if they have a coin counter. This will allow you to quickly convert coins to cash at no cost or to deposit the amount into savings.

Note: If you are *wise*, you will assess your coins before depositing. Certain coins are worth more than their actual face value. I have had pennies worth $2 or rare nickels worth more. You can make a *Dollar Decision* to keep or sell.

Save to *save*.

What I mean by this is: Reduce daily costs and expenses to find "extra" or "hidden" dollars to add to your savings accounts.

Although you generate income in the form of interest, your bank account should be separate from your other investments. If you have $17,441.12 in a retirement account, you do not have this much money saved.

Diversify your savings.

Diversification is all about breaking your money up and spreading it out. Putting it in different places for the same purpose: to grow and make more of itself.

Keep several baskets for your eggs. Whether a matter of preference or ignorance, many people only have one bank account. While I would not advise this, it is your decision. Please choose wisely.

CHAPTER 7
THINK
SMALL

DOLLAR DECISION$

CHAPTER 7
THINK SMALL

It seems almost everything is accessible these days. For this reason alone, we think we can have anything and everything we want. And sometimes two of each! We are guilty of accumulating more than we actually need. And in most cases, we didn't really even want most of our belongings as much as we thought. Dreaming big will motivate you towards wealth, but hard work and sacrifices accompanied by good financial goals will get you there.

The strongest advice I could offer anyone wanting to improve their financial condition is to "think small." Although you see yourself getting out of debt slowly, but surely, continue to live far below your means. If you have recently earned a $5,000 pay increase, don't go out and buy things and splurge. Keep living like you have for the last several months. If you were eating syrup sandwiches for lunch, don't move up to bologna just yet.

The strategy comes when we condition our minds to live without the things we want and don't really need. Soon, we will be able to save lots of money and when we are able to dine out or enjoy a mini-vacation it is far more enjoyable.

When I began this journey to change my financial health, I thought long and hard about how people in other countries live. In some countries, a person could live like a king for just a few dollars a day. Yet, in our country the average person lives off $10 (or more) a day.

When we minimize our lifestyles and expenses we simplify our lives and maximize the quality of living. It cannot be overemphasized; our expenses should not exceed our earning. Whether we make $100 a week or $10,000, this still applies.

Living Within Your Means

What does this even mean? Although this is so cliché, I have often asked myself if I even understood. When we live within our means, we buy things we can afford. Our expenses are managed by our income. When my lifestyle that I foolishly built forced me to survive on a paycheck-to-paycheck prayer, I knew that I needed to live far below my means of income and resources.

We will never get ahead if we are always striving to break even. If we are proud of ourselves for being just moderately broke, we need to develop new strategies. It is huge progress that we no longer have bouncing checks and a bank statement of overdraft fees, but we must not reward ourselves just yet. The reward will come after the sacrifice.

REDUCING COSTS AND EXPENSES

It's enough trying to make ends meet. Do not pay twice. Make a budget and stick to it. Automate your bill payments. Do not pay late fees or unnecessary charges for bank overdrafts. Save money, time, and resources.

Save on utilities.

Turn off lights and appliances you aren't using.

Stop running water and running water and running water. Plug the sink when shaving. Resist the urge of leaving the faucet running while brushing and flossing.

SETTLE FOR LESS

Do you need five bedrooms?

Do you need two cars?

Do you need a home with a kitchen and two dining areas?

Do you have items you have purchased only to store in closets and storage?

As a single person, do you absolutely need a 2,000 plus square-foot home right now?

It is not a sign of failure to cut back or scale down. Downsizing our housing or simply adjusting our lifestyles is not a step down. It is actually a step up. It helps us go through with these wise decisions when we remain focused on the greater picture. We must remember why we are making such great sacrifices.

Dining Options

Give yourself a per diem, if you must eat out. Place twenty $20 bills in an envelope. Make it a challenge to spend $5 or less a day.

Beverage Options

Consider changing your drink orders. Whether you purchase soft drinks from a store, vending machine or drive-thru, they cost. And whether you purchase alcoholic beverages from a pub or corner store, these expenses continue to pile up. Cutting the case of beer and 24 pack of soda a week is a good *money move*.

Transportation

Plan your driving. If you live 18 miles from your job and the market is a mile from there, shop then. Do not go home, change clothes for comfort, and return while wasting gas and time.

Entertainment Options

The road from being broke to becoming wealthy does not have to be unreasonable. It does us good to be entertained and to enjoy life's pleasures as often and we possibly can. There are countless available resources that provide inexpensive entertainment alternatives.

Local Public Library

I know I have mentioned this already, but I cannot emphasize enough.

Many years ago, after paying my last $140 cable bill I could not do it anymore. There were other reasons I cut it. I wanted to become more disciplined and I could not do so by spending all of my time on the couch watching TV. I certainly couldn't save money while paying $1,680 a year and $8,400 after five years. I canceled my services all together. It wasn't too much later that I canceled my Netflix, Hulu and Amazon subscriptions and took advantage of less expensive options.

The local library became my entertainment one-stop. Up to 10 DVDs could be checked out daily, including the latest selections. Almost everything that was in the Redbox or on cable was available at no charge. Streaming services and digital downloads were available, for free!

And after all, a library is for books. The latest best-sellers and classics were within my reach and if not, the branches in other cities would locate the books for me.

This was not a hard *Dollar Decision* for me. This one strategy has helped me save bundles of money that I was able to use to further pay off my debt. One of my greatest assets has been my library card.

Bargain Shopping

You better shop around. Try not to make large purchases without comparing prices. Saving $20 of $200 is $20 you did not have to spend.

Cellphones

Drop down to the basic plan for cellphone services. If you are a high-volume caller and texter take advantage of wi-fi options and services. If you are an Apple user, using *Message FaceTime* and *FaceTime Audio* can save cellular data and keep dollars in your pocket.

If your job provides a cellphone or you just don't need one anymore, cancel your service. If your carrier wants to be difficult and charge early-termination fees, ask them to suspend the service until the actual last day of the contract.

Do you still need a residential landline? If you have a cellphone and internet service, consider canceling the service. I was paying close to $40 a month for my home phone. Call waiting and few other features pushed it up to over $55 a month. After canceling, I now save $660 which could be better invested elsewhere.

Coupons

It is fun for many to spend hours hunting and collecting coupons only to spend another several hours organizing. I love that idea. It supports your financial plan and you will be strategically saving a lot of money. If you do not want to make a hobby of couponing, there are many apps that you can use. Look it up.

Bartering

If your attorney needs a fence repaired and you need a legal document drafted and stamped by the Clerk of Court, make a fair exchange. You repair the fence. The attorney will not charge you and you will not charge the attorney. Everyone's happy and you both saved money.

Skip the vacation. Build a sanctuary.

Occasionally, we want to escape our lives and lifestyles so we retreat to another state or country. It helps to get away and reset. This isn't a problem. The problem comes when we are forced to leave home and spend astronomical amounts to find peace. Own your house but continue to invest in your home. Rather than spending $6,500 each year visiting Costa Rica, bring Costa Rica to you. If you visit the Hilton several times a year for the sheets, buy your own. If you love the Palm trees in Miami, drop a few in your backyard for you to stretch out under. If you loved the hammock in Puerto Rico, get your own. Build your own retreat. Your own sanctuary. Paint the walls to add serenity. Create your own mini-spa in your bathroom. Hack your lighting to create a mood that relaxes you. Candles and aroma. Give it a try. If you still feel the need to travel, plan ahead. Far ahead of time. This will help you save and get the least expensive flights and preferred lodging. And forget buying worthless souvenirs and eat brown bag lunches rather than eating three meals a day while vacationing.

Gratitude

Thankfulness helps more than you would believe. I try to remain content, knowing that life could be so much harder. There is someone hoping for a matching organ donor that is willing. Another has lost every member of his or her family in one accident. Someone woke up this morning in their right bed, but not their right mind. I remind myself that I must check my total wealth regularly, not just my financial net worth. Both are equally important.

Take inventory of all the things that you value that you did not buy with money. Showing gratitude conditions us to be thankful for the things we have. If we don't get the new shoes or the designer bag, it's okay. Whether we consider ourselves *blessed* or fortunate, we have enough.

Being grateful is not just about showing thanks; it is about being so thankful that you show kindness. When we are truly thankful for what we have, we want to either appreciate these things or give to those who are less fortunate.

Giving helps us understand that "our stuff" is not "our substance." *Things* do not make us. Our character does. We no longer have the mindset of the broke, but the wealthy. We don't focus on greed and how we can impress others.

When we make it a routine to reflect daily on how fortunate we are, we are compelled to give. And in return, our generosity *always*, and I do mean *always* pays us far more than we've given.

CHAPTER 8
INCREASE INCOME AND POTENTIAL EARNING

DOLLAR DECISION$

CHAPTER 8
INCREASE YOUR INCOME AND POTENTIAL EARNING

Unless you have a hot product that sells, it is wise of us to invest in ourselves.

"Dress for the job you want, not the one you have." How many times have we heard this? While we have heard it too much, we have listened too little. The workplace seems to have changed from a corporate climate to a casual atmosphere. Years ago, when we thought about how a professional setting looked we would think of men in pinstriped suits with power ties and women in black designer heels with skirts and pant suits. Now it seems that the office workweek consists of five "Casual Fridays." The coworker with the jeans and t-shirt. The tennis shoes and flip-flops. Don't be foolish. If you aspire to be promoted or become a boss anywhere one day, don't wear casual clothes to work. While success is a simple formula it is not easy. It requires effort and lots of it.

Your appearance may not tell me everything about you, but it tells me everything I need to know. The way you look is not all about attractiveness and acceptance. The way we present ourselves tends to reveal how disciplined we are. Again, choosing to market yourself has the potential of increasing your opportunity, which increases your wealth and earning ability. This is a *Dollar Decision*.

And please note: Church clothes and 'Sunday best' are not always workplace attire.

Shoes

If you have more sneakers than dress shoes, and you are not an athlete, you need to reevaluate. You can't judge a book by its cover, but you can judge a professional by his or her shoes.

Gentlemen, polish your shoes and have your soles repaired as needed. Going sockless may always be in style, but it has no place in the workplace.

Ladies, invest in conservative shoes appropriate for the workplace. You would be surprised what your male supervisors pay attention to. Your mature female superiors are wondering why you wore white after Labor Day. They could even be wondering why you did not wear stockings.

Male supervisors are wondering why you didn't put on lotion. Or, they may wonder why you started removing your nail polish last night and stopped in the middle of doing so. Yet, you still wore peep toed pumps!

Offensive Clothing

Do not wear common logos, clothes with controversial messages and themes, or sports paraphernalia to work. Many have blown opportunities for petty reasons. If your supervisor's eyes turn red at the thought of the Dallas Cowboys, do not wear Dallas paraphernalia to work. Besides, the NFL isn't making any money for you. Who lost the Super Bowl? I don't care, but someone does.

Clemson or Carolina?
Someone in upper management would literally curse you out if you said a word against Auburn or Alabama.
Stay away from wearing anything that suggest questionable themes or views. The workplace is not the place to wear shirts or tags with Malcolm X, BLM, Dixie Flags, etc. Don't give anyone a valid reason to judge you or prejudge you. It sounds

immature and even imaginary, but this is real. Employers will deny you opportunities and promotions because of your affiliations. Be wise.

Do not wear Greek fraternity and sorority paraphernalia to work. This is not "School Daze." If you are going to an interview or to negotiate a multimillion dollar deal, be neutral. Remove the pin. Carry the black umbrella instead. Take off the frat hat before entering the building. Be proud of your strong tradition and exemplify your organization's values. But, do not wear them. It could cost you.

Wash and Press Your Clothes.

Invest in a good iron, ironing board, scorch guard and starch. Dry clean garments, such as suits, blazers, and ties as needed. Don't go anywhere wrinkled.

Note: If you work in a professional setting and wear clothes that do not need to be ironed, you're already doing it wrong. Try again.

GROOMING AND HYGIENE

Cleanliness

Practicing good hygiene is major. Wash thoroughly. Showering or bathing removes "personal" smells. While it has been for many years a rule of thumb to wash twice a day, many shorten to one. If you wash only once a day, remember to wash in the morning before you go to work. Although you have only been in a bed for 8 hours or less, a lot can go on in certain places. And I assure you, a sink bath and lotion won't wash it away. Deodorant and body sprays won't cover it up.

Cologne & Perfume

Do not wear too much cologne or perfume. It would be considered an offensive odor. Whether you work in an office, in a restaurant, or in a factory, do not wear too much "smell-good."
Upsetting those with allergies or those that simply hate the smell of cheap fragrances will dodge you. In time, they will make sure they never find you in their presence.

Wash your hands after putting on cologne or perfume. We should do this to be considerate. On the contrary, it is very inconsiderate to shake hands with colleagues and coworkers and leave them smelling you all day long.

COMMUNICATION

Watch your mouth!

It is a pitfall. Cursing may seem harmless to some, but I assure you, it offends professionals. Using offensive language highlights your lack of self-control and not to mention your limited vocabulary. Although, I know a few people who are beyond brilliant, but use profanity in every other sentence. As you would expect, they are not in my personal circle. No, I would not hire or recommend them for any job.

Ol' Time Religion

Do not play loud music of any kind at work. I have worked with several people who felt that playing gospel or inspirational music and sermons aloud was their form of ministry. I am no preacher, but it is said that "the best sermon is the one lived." *But y'all don't hear me though.*

Smile.

This will probably sound silly, but always wear a smile. And a real one at that. It will take you places aggressors and intimidators cannot go.

The Firm Handshake

Yes, it's still relevant. Male. Female. It makes no difference. When you shake a person's hand, mean it. No Jell-O shakes only firm grips.

Make eye contact.

Whether during an introduction or an interview look the speaker in the eye. If you are in a meeting or a training, actively pay attention. While this may be the multitasking age, give your full attention and eye contact to whoever controls the floor. Your mobile device can wait.

If looking someone in the eye makes you feel awkward, practice until you can do it comfortably.

WRITTEN COMMUNICATION

Whether job and loan applications or formal request, type it. Sign in blue or black ink. You will be evaluated by your written communication and presentation. If it is a job application, this is a part of your interview. This tells the reviewer whether you are lazy or resourceful. Your potential supervisor can gain insight on what type of employee you are likely to be simply by viewing the presentation of your completed application and resume.

Do not send religious-toned emails during work or chain letters with humorous undertones.

Choose appropriate email names (i.e.bigboy44@coldmail.com,44lulGanksta@cmail.com,RebelDixieChik@newlove.com, etc.

Meeting Protocol

All deals aren't made on the golf course. Bosses need to be able to handle business without any gimmicks. If you ever plan to become a leader and want someone to pay you for doing so, learn *Robert's Rules of Order*. Know how to run a meeting.

Exercise wisdom daily to protect your greatest investments.

Every day you leave home and go to work, understand you are protecting your investments/assets. Your house, your spouse, relationships and future. Don't throw it all away just to prove a point to someone.

Mind Your Manners

Manners are not old-fashioned. Courtesy is timeless. Always be a lady or gentleman in the breakroom, boardroom, or bedroom. When you are really serious about running things, you can even be a lady or gentleman in battle. There are rules to engagement.

Smile and be polite. Say "please" and "thank you." Even "yes ma'am" or "no sir." This isn't just a southern thing. Kindness is universal.

Brush up on your business and dining etiquette. Using table manners, including knowing which utensil is considered the salad fork, will score points when it comes to business. It shows potential partners and employers how polished you are.

Don't take your Home to Work.

Sure, you have disciplined yourself not to take work home. But do not take your home to work. Do not bring your children to work (or nephews, nieces, or pets)

This may gain graces of female coworkers and employees, but your leadership team will not be impressed.

Never handle a private matter publicly.

Whether you are a brick and mortar business owner or not, you are a business owner. You are a corporation. You generally provide a service and get money in exchange. Do not damage your reputation or blow your next promotion over personal matters. I make a habit of reminding myself that my feelings don't make me any money. My skills paired with professionalism does. When handling business, it is not about us. It's about the money and getting the job done.

Set Boundaries. Period.

Males and females. Don't be branded by others by association. Let your work and character speak for you.

Discipline will separate you from the crowd, but you must separate yourself from the few. Be friendly. Comradery is admirable. But remember, you go to work to make money, not friends.

Social Drinking

We live in a society filled with double standards. Women, certain types of males can be dishonest, disorderly and downright disrespectful in the workplace and *still* land a promotion. You could sip on one half-empty glass of wine and it could cost you your promotion and your credibility. It does not matter whether drinking alcohol is legal, ethical, or moral. Your job's Christmas party is not the time or place to end your career.

My advice to any professional has always been to focus on where you intend to go in life. Try not to waste too much time trying to prove what is or isn't fair.

Repair your credit.

Eliminate your debt as quickly as possible. Fine, but what does this have to do with increasing income or earning potential? Employers have the right to review credit reports as an evaluation tool. This tells a lot about your integrity. It reveals how responsible and accountable you are for your actions. Whether they have the right to use this information against you isn't the issue. The concern is: Will they use this information against you and when?

You started at entry-level and worked your way up to management. Do not let this be the only reason you were not offered the $200k leadership position.

IMPROVE YOUR HEALTH AND WELLNESS TO MAKE YOURSELF MORE MARKETABLE.

Remove bodily waste regularly.

We know to remove toxins from our bodies. We know that our bodies need sugar, but the right kind and amount. We know to drink a sufficient amount of water to replenish the body which helps us function at an optimal level. An unexpected upset stomach scenario can disrupt a schedule. We know this. But you would not believe how much having regular bowel movements affect everything from your mood to your daily performance. Research this topic yourself. If one has high anxiety levels, skin complications, loss of energy, weight issues, hair loss, offensive breath, and unclear thinking patterns, a regular bowel movement regime could be the cure. Anything that makes you healthier makes you productive. The more marketable, the more money. Don't overlook this one.

Sleep Well

The function of sleep is connected to every system of the human body. From diabetes or hypertension to heart disease or excessive weight gain; The lack of a six- to eight-hour sleep routine is almost always the culprit. I will not bore you with the science of sleep. I will not delve into how the hypothalamus (located inside the suprachiasmatic nucleus) affects our response to light and darkness while sleeping. You'll just have to take my word for it: If there is one action you can take to boost your overall health, performance, and keenness, it would be getting enough sleep.

STUDENT LOANS

Student Loans

Increasing our income is usually the easiest way to increase our cash flow and ultimately our wealth. Often, it is difficult to get a high-paying job without getting additional training and education. Sadly, bettering ourselves isn't free. Even education comes with a nice price tag. However, it is a good investment when coupled with the right opportunities.

If you have not taken out any student loans and do not have to, don't. If you can take advantage of scholarships and grants, it would be the better option. If student loans are necessary for you to reach your next level of success, go for it. But borrow the least amount needed to fund your education. Please, do not fall into the trap of using student loans as house, car, or department store loans.

Whenever we take out loans, we must be aware of what we are *getting into,* so we will know how to *get out of.*

Know your options for borrowing.

Know the difference between federal and private loans. Federal loans tend to be the better option. They don't normally require credit checks or qualifying FICO scores, unless it is a PLUS loan. If you qualify for a subsidized loan the government could pay your interest if you are enrolled in classes.

Private loans are a little different and should be avoided in most cases. You tend to spend more repaying the loans because the lenders are usually connected with banks, finance institutions, and credit unions. Being that they are solely in the business of *making* money, private student loans may not offer deferment or forbearance options. And you can just about forget about loan forgiveness programs, which we will discuss later.

Know that Free Application for Federal Student Aid (FAFSA) is the form that the United States *Department of Education* uses to determine who is eligible for financial aid.

Know that the limit you can borrow is determined by your FASFA.

Know how to apply for a FSA ID.

Know that in most cases you only become eligible for financial aid if you have a high school diploma or GED.

Know your benefits as a borrower.

Know your disadvantages as a borrower.

Know that you are responsible for repayment.

Know when to defer payments until you get a better paying job.
Know that when you borrow, you are paying to do so. It is called "borrowing and repaying with interest."

Know the difference between subsidized and unsubsidized student loans. The government pays the interests on subsidized loans while you are in school. With unsubsidized loans, you and only you are responsible for paying the interest.

Know that even after you finish your schooling there are tax credits/savings for those paying educational expenses and repaying loans used for these purposes.

Know that if you are in default because you tried college a time or two and never began repaying your prior student loans, you may not be eligible the next time around.

Know when to consolidate your loans and when not to. If you bundle several loans, would it be wise to pay off the smaller amounts? If you consolidate all of your past student loans, will it increase the time it would require to pay it off? Would the interest rate be higher on a larger amount? Could you possibly get lower payment amounts if you keep the student loans separate?

Know that you can, in most cases, negotiate your monthly student loan payment amount. You did know that, right?

Know the alternatives to repaying your student loans. Do you work in Education or Public Service? The federal government has several loan forgiveness programs waiting for those who qualify. In rural areas, there are many geographical regions and counties classified as "critical need/underserved" areas. An incentive for working in these high-need areas is forgiving student loans after serving the community for five years.

Know that certain non-profit and not-for-profit organizations are willing to allow former students to volunteer for a specified cause. In exchange, the organization forwards a payment of a predetermined amount to the student loan lender.

IMAGINARY REAL ESTATE

Increase your income with Creative and Intellectual Capital.

Wealthy people can't just let their dreams die. They do not sell their dreams, but they make sure that their dreams pay them. You are not likely to see an entrepreneur just give someone a piece of their mind. In this context, they do not just give good ideas away and certainly not for free. These are the types of people who know where the real money is. It's in "property." Intellectual property.

Imaginary real estate. It's invisible, but it exists. It is a property you can't just pull up to. It's huge yet it's portable. You pay no rent or taxes on it, but pays you royally, consistently and infinitely.

Look. I'll never be an NFL player. I will never get paid millions to run down a field for anything. Couldn't even if I wanted to. Even if I spent the rest of my life trying, it's not happening. Still, there is something that I have that the world is willing to pay me dearly for. We all have invisible assets that could pay us far more than any entertainer or athlete could even dream of making.

Think about it. Things that hold the most value can't be seen.

Love.

A solution.

Knowledge.

Influence.

A formula.

A good idea.

Passion.

Respect.

How a sweet song sounds and how it makes you feel.

How a good memory refuses to be forgotten.

A reputation.

A healing.

Purity.

Security.

Breath.

Life.

You are a real estate agent for your own invisible, intangible, intellectual property. Trademarks and trade secrets. Inventions and patents. Solutions to problems. A new fad or fashion. A design. A hairstyle or new method of styling hair. Waiting somewhere in your imagination, is an asset in the form of an idea. Convert these concepts to dollars or goodwill. Whatever you do, give it to the world and get something in return.

Let me offer some legal advice. If you have a billion-dollar solution or idea (related to your current employment) consider resigning before releasing to the market. Your employer may own the rights to your intellection property in certain instances.

The bottom line is: Ideas are our greatest assets; they are portable and can be sold an infinite number of times. Let that sink in.

CONTINUOUS PERSONAL DEVELOPMENT

Instead of consuming reality shows and sitcoms for two hours, learn and hone a skill daily.

Read often to gain knowledge. Convert this knowledge to opportunities. Opportunities become capital.

Assess yourself regularly. Know your skill set as well as your weaknesses.

PART II: LIFE HAPPENS

CHAPTER 9
GUARDING
THE NEST

DOLLAR DECISION$

CHAPTER 9
GUARD THE NEST

Life has few guarantees. One is this: Life comes with adversity. No one has ever hoped for calamity. No one has ever noted CANCER as a Christmas Wish List item. If the 327,000 people who lost spouses last year knew their 1-, 5-, or 50-year marriage would end, they probably wouldn't have even proposed. I've had close friends who had to casket shop for their elementary-age children.

If you have gone through anything critical, it changes you. It has a way of taking something from you. While adversity eventually tends to bring out the best in us, it brings the worst first. And we must prepare for it. A part of wealth is being able to protect the families that count on us to care for them. To feed and clothe them. We must have the financial resources in place to respond appropriately in difficult times.

Since life happens, we need all the financial assurance we can get. It's called *insurance*.

Types of Life Insurance

Do you need life insurance? Some do. Some don't. If you have a net worth of over $150k and you don't have a spouse and dependents, it may be no need. Given the same scenario, if you have a great spirit of generosity, you could possibly consider leaving your insurance payout to a foundation of choice.

Term Life vs Whole Life

Term Life is for a term, a limited amount of time. It could be 10 years or 20 years, but it will be specified. Whole life is "for your whole life" or what is left of it. A whole life has no expiration date as long as the benefactor lives. It pays out upon the death of the benefactor.

Insurance policies could cost more if you have less than a reasonable quality of health. Again, this is where our decisions about our health can cost us or pay us.

You buy a policy. As the policyholder, you have legally entered an insurance contract with the insurance company. A premium is the payment you submit to the insurance company usually monthly (or quarterly).

You need to know the language. If you look at your life insurance policy there is something called the "death benefit." It is the amount of money that the insurance company agrees to pay in the event of the policyholder's death.

The "beneficiary" is the family member or person that your policy states will get the money (or death benefit). In some cases, the beneficiary could die before or at the same time as the policyholder. The payout would then go to the next in line. These are called the contingent beneficiaries.

Health Insurance
Your health condition should be greatly important, particularly if you are a significant income earner in the family. And just the same, you want your family members to be provided the best health care possible. They deserve that. Health insurance affords us these comforts and protection.
The interesting thing with health insurance is there are so many options for healthcare plans. There are

HMOs, PPOs, HSAs, FSAs, and I am sure there are a dozen more that I am not aware of.

One reward of having a regular, full-time day job is the employer benefits. This is the value employment can bring. It isn't all about the pay. When it comes to fringe benefits, there are dollars that your employer pays on your behalf. In most cases with health insurance, the employer shares the cost of the premiums. It may appear expensive when you look at your paystub, but just imagine if you had to pay 100% of your price of health insurance coverage.

Copays are upfront, flat costs you pay a provider when you visit the doctor/specialist.

A deductible is the money that you pay the provider before your insurance company pitches in dollars.

Beware: Every service or procedure isn't covered by your insurance. This means, even if you've reached your out-of-pocket maximum, you could still pay more.

Property Insurance

You've worked too long and too hard to own your home and its contents. There are a few things to keep in mind regarding protecting these assets.

- Know the amount of coverage you have on your home. Should you have extreme damage, how much would the payout be if you have to replace personal items? Aside from the cash value, how much replacement cost coverage do you have if your house was completely destroyed?

- Know which types of claims have the potential of raising your premiums which causes the cost of the property to rise but not the value. This is not a good thing.

- Always take yearly inventory of your personal items located in the home. I've seen people take photos along with a list and upload to the Cloud. Keep these records in a safe place. Once, I had a situation causing me to file a claim. I produced serial numbers for my computers and appliances. I was issued a check from my insurance company immediately. Had I not produced good records, it could have been difficult to get my personal belongings replaced.

Insurance isn't all about protecting our belongings. It's also about protecting ourselves from liabilities. If a neighbor cuts her leg in your living room, you could be legally and financially responsible for the personal damage. What if your dog bites your child's play mate? Property insurance could help resolve these types of situations.

Retirement Planning

Making the decision not to work is one that seems lifetimes away. But it's not. Retirement is a milestone but it isn't a reward. Retirement is no more of a reward than death or taxes. Still, we must prepare for it. Retirement is not simply about not working. It is about having substantial resources to sustain yourself until death. If you're like me, you want to live as long as you possibly can. So, we need to make plans to enjoy a 30-year retirement without changing the quality of our lives. I refuse to work for over 25 years only to know I cannot have adequate health care or shelter. I will not retire and tell my grandchildren I can't fly to their graduations because I cannot afford to.

How much will I need?

I'd ask where you plan to live. Will you still have dependents? Health concerns? There are factors to consider.

How long will your dollars stretch? $200k in 40 years may be worth less than half the amount due to inflation.

If millennials will need over $2M for retirement alone, where would one get that money? Even with hefty contributions, it would almost take miracle to make and save that kind of money.

Perhaps you would want to participate in a deferred compensation program, such as a 401(k), just for the tax shelters and long-term investment. Well, what's a 401(k) really about? It is a type of retirement savings plan. If you participate, a part of your paycheck is stored away in this account. The benefit is some of this money is taken away from what the government would've taken for taxes. So, you are being rewarded for "paying yourself." As your money is deposited into your 401(k) it begins to grow because it is bundled with other contributors' money in a way. The beautiful part of it all is your contributions are tax-deferred.

The government will not tax you on it while you are building your wealth.

When should I begin saving for retirement?

Start today if you have not. It is never too soon.

GUARD YOUR IDENTITY

Protect Your Information

It would be foolish to incriminate one's self in a written publication, so I'll just say I knew a hacker in my younger years. It's a good thing people think characters like *Mr. Robot* are completely fictional. I suppose it would make us sleep a little better at night.

Protect your personal information. It is true: If a hacker or identity theft wants your information, he or she will get it, but don't make it easy for them.

Passwords and PINs. Pin codes and access numbers that are the first four of your street address or birthdate. How about the last four of the Social Security Number? The child's first name followed by the current year. Password1234. I've seen it all. Come on, it's too easy.

These guys have sniffers and scanners that can pull your encrypted data from the network while you are on the Facebook Messenger app and take all the information they need.

Consider these tips to protect your identity:

Change your passwords every 30 days.

Check your bank statements and credit reports regularly.

Don't throw your receipts away. Shred them.

Don't open every email you receive in your inbox. If it's suspicious, don't open it. It's enough to link a spy server to your computer. The link you click on in the email could help someone remotely install a key logger on your computer or mobile device. They will have a written record of everything you type. Passwords. Text messages. Everything!

If you still order checks, don't. Have your checks, debit and credit cards mailed to your local branch. Picking them up from the bank is safer. Don't think that people don't check *YOUR* mailbox occasionally. You'd be surprised what people do when you're not looking. Protect yourself. Your information is just as valuable as your physical assets.

Death

Death can come unexpectedly. Yet, life goes on with or without us. The loss of a family member can be devastating and missing them is just the beginning. For many, dying is a financial disaster. Whether leaving a financial burden or being left with one, it must be dealt with. A part of our financial planning should always include death.

Funerals cost a lot. If you've experienced the death of a family member, you know that most of us want to give our loved ones a decent burial. The average funeral costs about $10,000. Who just has this kind of money in a shoe box?

The expenses seem to keep adding up:

Embalming services.
Programs and keepsakes.
Death certificates and obituary notices.
Hair and viewing clothes.
Caskets and flowers.
Cash advances for third party services.
Hearses and limos.
The cemetery plot.
Work absences due to making funeral arrangements.
Job loss due to excessive absences due to making funeral arrangements.

I do not have the right to tell you how to manage your money or how to make funeral arrangements when the time comes. Whether planning yours or a loved one's, we should make *Dollar Decisions*. With or without a paying life insurance policy, like a wedding, there is life after the ceremony. If you decide to spend $20,000 to honor the dead, much respect to you. But please, understand you will need $20,000 and much more to recover from this life interruption. Maybe you would consider less expensive burial alternatives.

There are traditional funeral services and nontraditional. One can cut costs by eliminating embalming services. One can have a direct burial without the services. Also, one can have a family member cremated and have a memorial in place of funeral services and burial. Just be prepared.

WILL & TESTAMENT

A certain proverb reveals that a good person not only leaves an inheritance for their children, but even their grandchildren. Financially wise people do this. It doesn't matter that they will not be alive to witness this. They understand that they are responsible for making plans for their assets many years after death.

In my home state, South Carolina, the Code of Laws outlines what happens in the event of a person dying without a written and executed will. An attempt is made to transfer the assets and property to the next of kin. After these remedies have been exhausted, and no kin is found or lawfully determined, the property is handed over to the State.

Write a will immediately. Find two witnesses and have them sign immediately after you do. Make copies. Give copies to your attorney, your spouse/and or administrator and leave in a conspicuous place in the event you and your spouse expire simultaneously. Will and Testament forms can be found at your public library. Or, just schedule an appointment with your attorney. By now, you should have one.

GET YOUR EMERGENCY BLANKET.

Not-so-good things will happen. It isn't just the life crises that throw your finances off. It isn't always the laptop or wardrobe we charged that keeps us in debt either. Most of the time it's the new tires you needed. The blown engine on the vehicle and the warranty just ended last month. It's those things and incidents we can't avoid.

An emergency blanket is an account that is used only for unexpected costs and expenses. Most financial advisors suggest three to six months of expenses to keep you afloat in case of a setback, such as losing a job or long-term illness. This will seem overwhelming at first, but I assure you, when you start, it gets easier. Start with several dollars and work your way to a hundred. Continue to add to the account. If you have dip into it, always remember to pay yourself back. If you don't use it, even better. There's just something about the security of knowing it's there.

As you save and cut monthly expenses, make it your business to transfer money to your emergency account. Now you aren't depending on credit cards and high interest rates to take care of you. This is a *Dollar Decision*. Nice move.

Remember, emergencies only.

Convenience is not an emergency. "Broke" is not an emergency. Want isn't an emergency, neither is greed. It will be tempting to go for your emergency blanket when you want the new purse or new car down payment, but this isn't the fund to touch. Leave these dollars alone.

CHAPTER 10
MONEY MISTAKES

DOLLAR DECISION$

#1: MONEY MISTAKE
Marrying a fiscally foolish spouse.

Think two or three times about marrying someone with excessive debt. Her debt will become your debt. His baggage and liabilities will become yours. Serial dating fiscally foolish partners is just as unwise and far costlier.

#2: MONEY MISTAKE
Spending a fortune on an engagement ring and wedding, but investing little in the marriage and future financial security.

Okay, we can look at this two ways.

First, if your future spouse is overly materialistic, this should make you reconsider. If a future spouse wants you to spend several thousand dollars that you don't have, before saying, "I do," it could be a good sign that she wants your money and wants to be significant. It is a strong possibility that she does not even want to marry you. You just happened to be the one that asked her. On the other hand, especially for traditional females, if a guy won't spend several thousand dollars on a ring and wedding, he may not be *the ONE*. It would make plenty sense for a business woman to think aloud: "If a man can't spend that kind of money on the woman of his dreams, he may not see me as a worthy investment." Furthermore, if he cannot afford a ring, how can he properly care for a wife and family for many years to come? Ladies, this too could be a sign to run.

#3: MONEY MISTAKE
Cheating. Period.

If you are married, whether it is morally irresponsible or unethical is beside the point. It is just not a good *Dollar Decision*. You are wasting money, time, and energy. In time, your current assets will slowly become liabilities. It is not a good *Dollar Decision* to make a great investment in building your palace only to tear it down.

#4: MONEY MISTAKE
Being too traditional

I understand your great-grandfather had 7 children. He worked two jobs while your great-grand mother stayed at home and kept the place. That was in the early 1900s. The economy and the value of the dollar was much different then. And no offense but, he died before he saw 50 years old. God bless the dead. Sir, you are no less of a man for allowing your wife to work and help generate income for the home. If you are making $200k a year and it works for you, fine. But please, do not let your ego and your $40k salary job cause you and your family to suffer financially.

#5: MONEY MISTAKE
Being Nontraditional

Ma'am, I understand that you can do anything that a man can do and just as good I might add. But, have you had a conversation with your husband about going back to work? He quit his job to focus on his passion of fantasy football. That interest just disappeared. Then he wanted to become a professional golfer. Exactly. After two years and $16,000 of hobby-related debt, he has since retired from the sport and is currently at home, right now, researching becoming a full-time YouTube celebrity. Need I say more?

#6: MONEY MISTAKE
Financial Unfaithfulness

Yes, you read it right- cheating when it comes to finances. He didn't have the money to visit your parents at Thanksgiving, yet he purchased new golf clubs the following week. She forgot to pick up groceries on Thursday night but she remembered to stop by Kohl's and hide the $400 worth of clothes in her car trunk. When her husband's in the shower she sneaks the new threads into her closet.

Spouses must communicate and be open with their intentions and financial plans. This could later cause other problems in the marriage. So, no secret savings accounts. No hidden credit cards. No stealing money out of her pocketbook. Be financially faithful!

#7: MONEY MISTAKE
Cosigning

Only cosign on a loan for a house or an automobile (or any purchase) if you intend on assuming the payments one day. By law, you become legally responsible for the debt. Cosigning for your roommate may not be the best idea. If you are serious about becoming and staying debt-free, do not cosign.

#8: MONEY MISTAKE
Having a "Buy-mindset" rather than a "Sell-mindset"

We are highly creative beings. We were made to create, yet we still want to be consumers. We wait for new products and newly innovated services to come out just so we can go broke buying them.

Please understand that you have multimillion dollar dreams in your heart right now. Your ideas and visions, you've neglected. You have at least a dozen ideas in your head that could generate dollars for you if you would only materialize those thoughts into reality.

The world is waiting on something only you can give it. In exchange for your product or service, the world will pay you. I promise. Don't be lazy. But most of all, don't be selfish. Go to "sell!"

#9: MONEY MISTAKE
Bouncing Checks

Aside from fees for overdrafts and insufficient funds, pushing a bad check is a crime. Writing a check including an amount and your signature is your promissory note that you are personally guaranteeing payment of those funds. If those dollars are not in your account and the check does not clear, this could potentially be a huge problem for you.

#10: MONEY MISTAKE

Thinking a grace period will always save you

Repay debt in a timely fashion. There are some loans that have grace periods and you do not

get penalized with interest you are obligated to repay. However, this does not apply in every situation.

Pardon my colloquialism, but this ain't church. In most banking and lending institutions there is no "grace period." Interest and penalties come every day of the week, including Sundays.

#11: MONEY MISTAKE
Still 'Keeping up with the Joneses

Have you ever met the Joneses? Please believe, they are not concerned with you or with what you've got. Secondly, and pardon my colloquialism [again], but "they broke." The *Dollar Decision* Philosophy inspires us to focus on our own financial goals and vision of *Wealth and Plenty*.

Personally, I have never wanted a boat, motorcycle, or several pairs of high-priced alligator skin boots. So why would I spend money on things I don't want or need to impress people?

You are the boss of your dollars. You tell them where to go and they go.

Don't let the interests of others control your spending.

Build and maintain a lifestyle that you desire most. The Joneses don't matter.

#12: MONEY MISTAKE
Buying a Brand-New Car

What's this about buying a brand-new car and trading a vehicle as a down payment? If you have a well-maintained vehicle and it is paid for, keep it. It is an asset. If anything, drive it or sell it yourself. The dealer could take the car that you worked so hard to pay off and sell it themselves.

#13: MONEY MISTAKE

Expecting work to finance your romance

I assure you, it will cost you more than you're willing to pay. Many men have poured dollars down the drain over a DM photo, short skirt, nice legs and a smile. And many women have done the same.

Please, do not trade your passing bar exam score, teaching or welding certificate for a fling. Damaging your credibility can put you at risk of losing opportunities for advancement and even employment. In many cases, lust can cost us our freedom.

#14: MONEY MISTAKE

Making purchases without considering the "true cost"

The bulky projection television I couldn't afford. Charged $2000 to the credit card. Didn't finish paying for it until everyone in America had a flat screen. With interest and penalties for late payments, I paid over $3000 for the oversized piece of junk.

The automobile with the price tag of $25,550. It was within your price range. You said you'd never pay over $30k for a car. Yet, after paying it off, with an APR of 17%, you actually paid $40,923.98.

The refrigerator with the ice maker your neighbor is renting to own. The price was $1,500. With an interest rate of 60%, your neighbor is paying over $2,400 for the appliance.

The $90 George Strait Concert tickets you charged actually costed you $174 after added interest. Well, never mind. It *was* George Strait.

#15: MONEY MISTAKE

Making hasty, uninformed decisions

The greater the opportunity, the greater the risk. So, the greater the cost, the more information and time is required to make a good decision.

I am never compelled to make a life changing decision in a matter of seconds. This is isn't wise.

#16: MONEY MISTAKE
Using a payday loan as a solution for poor budgeting

Payday Loans? This is an easy one. Don't do it. You'll pay more in interest that you would towards the principal. The average lender charges about $18 for every $100. Are you serious? This is like a 425% interest rate! No, thank you!

#17: MONEY MISTAKE
Using your savings for startup capital

Why would you use your savings to start a business? You've already paid taxes on it. Besides, if you need cash immediately, you can't liquidate a business as quickly especially if the money's tied up in equity. Not equity, but even more plainly, *debt.*

Become creative with finding money to start your business. Use the equity of another property or asset. Use it as collateral or use it to generate capital (money).

Find a venture capitalist or angel investor. Someone who either believes in your vision or sees value in your business plan so much to put up part or all funds.

For some reason, you may want to be the sole owner and do it yourself. Do this the next time around. Partner with an investor. He funds the whole business startup and you provide the knowledge and expertise. Negotiate the percentage of ownership. Your expertise and knowledge is worth something.

This is extra advice and it won't cost you anything but time:

Make sure that you know whether you want to own a business or run a business. Do you want to be a boss or a businessperson? Do you want to make a profit or do you want to have control?

Two things:

1. If cash flow is what you want, consider buying an up-and-running business or partner with someone. Don't exhaust your time and resources taking the risks if you don't have an abundance of assets already.

2. Seek part ownership, even a percentage. If you own 25% of a car wash you can generate a stream of income. Even if only $500 a week, that is $500 that you will get without even getting out of the bed in the morning. You will still have time to play with your dog and take your children to the park. On the other hand, if you owned the car wash, you'd work 7 days a week. You'd work long after the place closed. And then after paying employees and expenses, you'd probably be tired and still only make $500. Which is the better deal?

Oh, and if you decide to build a business make sure it can run efficiently with or without you there. If it does this and it generates cash flow, it's passive income. If you have to work your business day and night to get the cash, you're not doing it right.

You know how it's said: "It's not how much you make, it's what you do with it?"
Well, it's not about how much money your business makes. It's about how much profit you made.
Business isn't about breaking even.
Breaking even still leaves you broke!

I am not saying this to discourage you. Just be aware of what you are getting into and why.

#18: MONEY MISTAKE
Having "The Never-mind"

Having the "Never-mind". Having the belief that death will *never* come. I will *never* see retirement. I'll *never* have enough to save or to invest for long-term returns. Or, I *never* have enough to give. This type of thinking doesn't come from a mindset of wealth.

#19: MONEY MISTAKE

Holding grudges personally or professionally

Deciding to forgive and let go is a *Dollar Decision*. If our spending has a direct connection to our hearts and minds, we risk the chance of experiencing at least two hurtful things: The blocking our own prosperity; or the stifling our own generosity.

I challenge you to forgive your father that was never there. Forgive your mother who made mistakes that left you broken. Forgive your grandfather for dying. Forgive your siblings, exes, anyone including yourself. And who knows, those that you want nothing to do with may be the very ones that indirectly bring tremendous wealth and blessings one day. Becoming bitter is not anywhere on the roadmap to becoming wealthy.

#20: MONEY MISTAKE

Not Paying Taxes

Tax liens will mess you up. Ask me how I know. Not only can your paycheck be garnished but beyond the shameful docked pay, your credit score is damaged. Hustle and pay off the tax debt. Understand that it will more than likely remain on your credit report for 7 years. But remember, it's your responsibility.

Consider the "Fresh Start Program." Submit Form 12277 and request that the lien be withdrawn.

#21: MONEY MISTAKE

Not Knowing Your Value

When "keeping it real" is keeping you broke, stop it right now. When being true to the neighborhood is bringing you great losses, you must separate yourself. Call them. Text them goodbye. Or, simply never have contact again. If your friends are not going where your life is going, leave them. If they care about you half as much as you think they do, they will understand.

May I take my time on this one? This one will really improve your life drastically if you are willing to digest this.

How much is your time worth right now? Can you afford to waste time? Maybe you think so. Your time is and *should* be valuable to you, but don't expect it to be valuable to anyone else. When your college drinking buddy calls you at 3 a.m. asking you to pick him up from a bar 20 miles away, you understand that both you and your time are too valuable. Wealthy people don't have time to waste on anything.   Their time is well spent on worthwhile financial and emotional investments.

One of the turning points of my career was when I realized I didn't have time for everyone. I learned to say "no" to people and it felt good. I stopped wasting my time, energy or money unnecessarily. Because bottom line, it was only costing me. I was only their entertainment.

As your net worth increases and you begin generating wealth, you will have to begin denying access. You will have to cut friends and acquaintances off. We determine our value by how much access we allow. A multimillionaire does not receive text messages about memes all through the night. A 28-year old with two 2,000 square foot homes does not have time to gossip on the phone for hours. Your time is an opportunity for potential earning. Do not allow people to drain your dollars by draining your time and creativity. Spend less time catering to people who don't respect your dreams. Instead, take that time and work towards bringing your vision to life. This is how you increase your value. Soon, your hourly rate could be $100, $1000, or more.

Most wealthy people were considered self-made. Didn't even come from money. However, when they generated their large sums of wealth, I assure you- they didn't do so by letting anyone waste their time.

Knowing how much you're worth tells *you* who and what is worth your time. One harsh reality is: Most of us actually get paid what we are worth. Even if we're paid no attention.

#22-: MONEY MISTAKE
Failing to save strategically for recurring expenses (Property Taxes and Anniversary, Birthday, and Christmas Gifts)

We know that our birthdays haven't changed since we were born. We also know on Christmas Eve that in three hundred and sixty something days, Christmas will be right back here again. The same is true for our anniversaries and loved one's special days. Why do we wait for a year only to be stressed about how we will buy gifts? I used to look forward to the holiday spirit, then, I would dread it because I was financially irresponsible. When I disciplined myself to plan and save dollars throughout the year, the holidays became far more enjoyable than I'd ever dreamed.

Open an additional bank account and set up the automation to save a few dollars a pay period. If not, get another jar. Push a $5 or $10 dollar bill a week in that bad boy. When it is time to pay house or car taxes or even gifts, it won't be such a strain on your pockets.

CHAPTER 11
WORTH
EVERY PENNY

DOLLAR DECISION$

Chapter 11
WORTH EVERY PENNY

By now we know that every decision is a *Dollar Decision*. Yet, every investment will not yield the same return. For some investments, we may never see a return. We will take many losses in this business of life. When making these types of decisions it all comes down to: who and what is worth your time, energy, and resources.

PARENTING

Deciding to have children weighs on martial satisfaction. That's just the truth. Are you ready for this? How much will children cost? Are you willing to push out hundreds of thousands of dollars? For most, for the love of the child every dollar spent would be a worthwhile cost. For others, raising children and managing a marriage would be too great of a burden. Let's face the fact that everyone isn't built for the business of family.

And that's fine if you decide this before you actually begin growing a family.

Jay and Rita's story reminds us that we must find wealth and not just riches. The beautiful couple wanted the best for their future family. They vowed that their children wouldn't grow up poor as they had. Jay became one of the youngest executives in his company and Rita became the second female and first Latino superintendent in the history of an unnamed school district. Finally, after financial preparation, the couple began trying for a child. An unsuccessful year turned to years. And years turned to hopelessness. Over twenty-two thousand dollars spent on fertility treatments, yet still, no baby.

At the age of 54, Rita just could not give up on the idea of raising a child. Long story short, it was financially and emotionally exhausting, but the Garcias held Baby Andy for the first time at 56 years old. My point is this: We need to make money, but chasing dollars won't make us happy in the end. Remember, money is all about funding your dreams and maintaining the lifestyle you've always wanted. Stay focused and don't you even think about giving up!

PENNY PHILANTHROPY

A man's gift makes room for him and brings him before greatness. It is not only our innate abilities or talents. Not even our willingness to share our gifts. It is about giving from our hearts.

Our generosity rewards us by providing more benefits to the giver than the recipient. While it reduces your stress, keeps you focused and humble, giving has a way of helping you put money into its proper place. Yes, I believe in the biblical and psychological sense of the Law of Reciprocity. I do believe that when you give and do good for others, it comes back to you many times over. I truly believe that when you have learned to give unselfishly without wanting anything in return, you are only steps from becoming a wealthy person. I can't explain it. I just believe it. I've seen it far too many times. The people that I know that will never go broke are the ones who simply cannot stop giving to others.

The beautiful thing about giving is, you don't have to give everything you've got. You don't always have to give an astronomical amount.

You don't have to donate hundreds or thousands. You can be a "Penny Philanthropist." Even *giving small* from a big heart can make a huge difference.

1. Donate items to those in need, directly or through a local organization like the Salvation Army.

2. Save pennies throughout the year and donate to a cause of your choice, every January.

3. Adopt a senior adult at an assisted living facility. Buy a pack of razors, rollers, socks, anything and drop off a few times a year.

4. Deliver goods to the local animal shelter. Paper towels, bleach, pet toys, and food tend to be appreciated. Usually, you can find a list of needed items on their website.

GIVE YOURSELF.

It seems selfishness has impaired our ability to show compassion. Our willingness to truly love our neighbors is often unseen. Every opportunity we are given to show compassion, we should do so. This was mentioned in a previous chapter of this book, but I thought the topic was worthy of being further discussed. I wanted to remind us, including myself, that deciding to demonstrate generosity is always a *Dollar Decision*.

CHAPTER 12
TAXES:
THE BIG
PAYBACK

DOLLAR DECISION$

CHAPTER 12
TAXES: THE BIG PAYBACK

Although we tend to dread taxes, they can actually help build wealth. Leveraging your taxes could help you generate dollars from nothing. There is actually a way to "make a dollar out of fifteen cents." It is all done with tax credits, deductions, and exemptions. Also, there are other strategies to get your "Uncle Sam" to be more generous.

Get an Extra Tax Refund

Request for Penalty Waiver

For the State of South Carolina, I completed Form C-530 which was still current at the time of this publication. It could vary from state to state, but you'll get the idea. I included my explanation on why I should be considered for a penalty waiver. I included that my employment was terminated after 13 years and that I had not yet regained employment. I submitted the request and within 30 days, the *Department of Revenue* mailed me a check in the amount of $823.16.

It worked. I knew I was on to something. I couldn't believe it, because I've never been lucky. I never win drawings and prizes or anything like that. Maybe, that is one reason why I don't believe in luck. And if this wasn't just a random blessing, it was a solution to a problem. This meant with the right formula it would work again.

To save some time, according to the law, I could do this for 3 years. I submitted another request and I was issued a nice check.

I then went after the Internal Revenue Service (IRS) with the same strategy. When you submit a request to the IRS to refund you those extra dollars for penalties, they consider what they call "reasonable causes". Reasonable causes include "fire, casualty, natural disaster or other disturbances, inability to find records, death, or illness."

"Chu-ching!" 'Got'em' again. I won't include my reason, but it was valid. This worked so well for me that I began taking the money that the government refunded me and applying to prior tax debt. I could not have been more inspired when I was later mailed a "Notice of Overpayment" from the *Department of Revenue.*

I did not learn this from a CPA or tax expert. I learned this from reading tax codes at the *Florence County Library* early one numbing Saturday morning in January. It costed me nothing but time and paid me more than I'd ever imagined.

For Better or for Worse: Marrying into a Tax Burden

Love is blind, but you aren't stupid. Marrying someone is the most important *Dollar Decision* you can make. If your spouse (who you thought was "rich") owes $75,000 in back taxes and you make the mistake of filing jointly, you will also be held legally responsible for the total amount.

When the IRS attempts to collect this debt, or intercept your tax refunds, consider submitting a Request for Innocent Spouse Relief (File Form 8857).

If you are the spouse with the tax burden, please be considerate and initiate this process on his or her behalf.

What Tax Bracket Are You In?

You have struggled in the past, but now you are making more money. You've done well for yourself. How's that working for you? Success is a blessing and a curse. When I first earned a six-figure salary I felt penalized for my achievements. No offense to the drug traffickers, money launderers, and white-collar criminals, but they don't pay taxes. And they make far more than a small-time guy like me. Be prepared for this.

As the fourth *Dollar Decision* principle states: *Wealth must be maintained.* Your wealth will be taxed. The more money you make, the more creative you'll have to become to protect it.

The key is to lower your taxable income. Itemizing deductions is an excellent start.

Home Improvement?

Certain renovation credits are available to you if you made changes to your house due to a medical issue. Energy-efficient credits are also available if you added items such as, solar panels and energy-efficient hot water heaters

Keep your receipts.

Earned Income Credit

This is an overlooked tax credit. I'm willing to bet you that the ones that bypass this option think that they don't qualify. It is viewed as a low-income credit but there are many who could take advantage. Maybe you earn a decent living but experienced a decrease in your income for a part of the tax year. Were you forced to take FMLA after illness or having a child? Were you forced to take a significant pay cut or lost employment in the middle of the year? This could be for you.

Note: If this slipped by you last year, you can always amend or include it within 3 years. Ask your tax advisor about this.

Child Care Credit

The average tax payer with dependents is aware of the code that states that tax credit is available for children (under the age of 13) receiving paid childcare services. However, many aren't aware of the fact that adult dependents are also covered under this code. If you are responsible for caring for an ill or disabled adult child, spouse or parent, you can and should take advantage of this tax benefit.

Good- for ~~Nothing~~ -Something

My parents, Bill and Pat, are incredibly generous individuals. Generosity is a value that they taught us by example. For many years, I have committed to giving at least 20% of my earnings. I knew that I could get a tax deduction for paying my 10% tithe to the church. But I didn't know that I could deduct the cost of everything I gave towards my other "penny philanthropic" efforts.

If you are like my father, you could benefit from this. He religiously provides landscaping for all the church's properties and to several citizens unable to care for their yards. The oil, gas and related expenses can be included and deducted as charitable gifts. But knowing *him*, he doesn't.

CHAPTER 13
WEALTH+PLENTY

DOLLAR DECISION$

CHAPTER 13
WEALTH AND PLENTY

Money simply isn't enough. A good life is about achieving reasonable balance between work and play and having the time, health and resources to enjoy the two. *Wealth and Plenty* is about our lifestyles being in harmony with our dreams.

You will have the wealth and resources to sustain you and your family until death and beyond.

You have built a lifestyle for your dreams; now *Wealth and Plenty* will reward you for your sacrifices.

You expect wealth and abundance and you have developed an appetite for it.

You have developed the ability to think short and long-term; in the present and the future.

Although you have missed opportunities, you are now better-prepared for greater ones.

You will grow from your failure. You will even profit from your mistakes.

We cannot excuse ourselves from adversity, but you are prepared if it comes.

The best years of your life haven't come and gone. You will enjoy *Wealth and Plenty* beginning today.

You will only acquire assets that create cash flow.

Money hasn't changed you, but you have changed the lives of your family and community. You have done *good for something*. You have been generous without expecting anything in return and it was *worth every penny*.

You will have financial security and emotional peace.

Conclusion

If I had any final words to share on making *Dollar Decisions,* it would read something like this:

Always make good decisions.

Maximize your minutes. Make the best use of your time. Multiply your options by maximizing your dollars. Make the best use of your resources. Make every moment count and enjoy it as best as you possibly can.

Take care of your mind, body, and spirit. It is your first and greatest investment.

Only take personal risks for greater rewards. If the risk outweighs the reward, don't take the chance.

Eliminate your debt. Repay all you owe.

Make it your business to increase your income each year. And then, each month, make more than the last.

Security is more important than the tax advantages owning a home provides. Pay the house off. Truly own it. Find other tax breaks. At least you'll never have to worry about finding a place to live. One less worry. One more reason to be happy.

Find a good spouse and take good care of him or her. Your family is your second greatest investment, but always your first financial priority.

Lastly, this book is for you and your determination to build a better life for yourself and the ones you love. May your life never be the same, but much more prosperous.

It was a pleasure writing this book for you.

Thank you kindly,

Andre Boyd

RESOURCES

DOLLAR DECISION$

DOLLAR DECISION$

LIFE PLAN

Live life and mean it.

EMOTIONAL ASSETS

List the full names of the five most important people in your life. Remember, you can only choose five.

_____
_____
_____
_____
_____

DAILY DISCIPLINE

What specific things will you do daily to accomplish your goals and fulfill your dreams?

_____
_____
_____
_____
_____

VALUES

Circle your most important values. Circle three only.

Abundance Affection
Appreciation Comfort
Education/Personal Development
Enjoyment, Entertainment, and
Excitement
Generosity, Charity, Making a
Difference
Good Health and Wellness
Marriage, Family, and Relationships
Resourcefulness
Security
Spirituality
Success and Significance

FINANCIAL GOALS

_____
_____

PENNY PHILANTHROPY (GIVING)CAUSE

What cause will you support or donate money to this year?

DREAMS

What are your life dreams? What will you look back at when you're old and be grateful about accomplishing or gaining?

191

THE DOLLAR DECISION
PHILOSOPHY
BUILDING YOUR WEALTH AND PLENTY

1
EVERY DECISION IS A DOLLAR DECISION.

Every decision will either cost us or pay us.

2
EVERY DOLLAR HAS A
PURPOSE.

A dollar's only purpose is to
multiply our options, by
increasing our Wealth and Plenty,
which ultimately improves every
dimension of our lives.

3
WEALTH IS NOT FOR
EVERYONE.

Wealth and Plenty are not obtained
by everyone; they can be obtained
by anyone disciplined and
determined.

4
WEALTH IS A HOUSE.

Wealth is a house. It must be built, secured, and maintained.

5
NEVER MAKE
"POOR" DECISIONS.

We may not always make the best
decisions, but we must always make
good ones.

⊕ **DOLLAR DECISION$**

Should I go through the hassle of establishing paternity for child support?

Should I start a business now or should I retire from my current place of employment in 30 years?

Should I get this tattoo on my neck? Should I spend my last 16 years of savings to get this tattoo removed?

Do I take care of my elderly or disabled parents? If so, should I take my parents in with my spouse and children?

Should I subscribe to long-term care insurance?

Should I sell shares of stock or should I keep them longer for a greater return?

Should I get married and risk everything I own being split with someone who could possibly leave me?

Should I leave my well-paying job to live my dream?

www.ingramcontent.com/pod-product-compliance
Lightning Source LLC
Chambersburg PA
CBHW070926210326
41520CB00021B/6823